Lobotomy

THUNDER'S MOUTH PRESS NEW YORK

LOBOTOMY

Surviving the Ramones

DEE DEE RAMONE

WITH VERONICA KOFMAN

Published by
Thunder's Mouth Press
An Imprint of Avalon Publishing Group Incorporated
161 William Street, 16th Floor
New York, NY 10038

Second edition

First Edition written with Veronica Kofman
Second Edition edited by Danny Weizmann

Previous edition published by Firefly Publishing in association with
Helter Skelter Publishing Ltd.

The publisher wishes to thank Erik Kahn
who was instrumental in getting this project going. N.O.

Library of Congress Cataloging-in-Publication Data

Ramone, Dee Dee.
Lobotomy : surviving the Ramones / by Dee Dee Ramone.
p. cm.
Originally published: Poison heart : surviving the Ramones.
Wembley, Middlesex : Firefly Pub., 1997.
ISBN 1-56025-252-9
1. Ramone, Dee Dee. 2. Ramone, Dee Dee—Drug use. 3. Ramones
(Musical group) 4. Rock musicians—United States Biography.
5. Punk rock music—History and criticism. I. Title. II. Title:
Surviving the Ramones.
ML419.R32A3 2000
782.42166'092—dc21
[B]
99-42130
CIP

Designed by Pauline Neuwirth, Neuwirth & Associates, Inc.

Manufactured in the United States of America

10 9 8 7 6 5 4 3

contents

Dee Dee Ramone thanks The Ramones, Ira Herzog, Michael & Sally at Herzog & Strauss, Seymour Strauss, Daniel Rey, Larry Schatz, Ed Steinberg, Seymour Stein, Harold Holloway, Dr. Finkel, Dr. Hanch, Stanley Bart, Western Union, Neil Ortenberg and Thunder's Mouth Press, and everybody who has stood by me in my life.

Dee Dee Ramone epitomizes the quintessential punk rocker.

In a time when rock stars have become neatly packaged products trading on twenty-five-year old ideas and music they neither originated nor improved on, Dee Dee stands as a reminder as to why rock & roll stars used to be so compelling—when rock stars actually meant something. I know it seems hard to believe now, but they did mean something once, a long, long time ago.

And the reason why they were so compelling, besides those cute haircuts and tight leather pants, was because they were sexy losers. Before the music, we only got to see these beautiful losers in newsreels and newspaper headlines after their spectacular crime sprees came to a screaming finish.

Charles Starkweather, the James Dean look-a-like who, along with his girlfriend, Carol Ann Fugate, killed her parents because they didn't approve of him, then went on a week-long killing spree across North and South Dakota (and became the subject of the movie, "Badlands") is the perfect example. The guy was a rock star. He had the look,

The Rock and Roll Crime Spree

LOBOTOMY

the hair, and the sneer. We knew him. We understood when he said, "Fuck it."

So when Elvis, Jerry Lee Lewis, Mick Jagger, Bob Dylan, Keith Richards, Jimi Hendrix, Keith Moon, and Janis Joplin all got up there and did the same thing, only to music, we knew who they were. They were sociopathic criminals who found a forum in rock & roll, and became overnight superstars, because we loved them for getting away with it.

DEE DEE RAMONE, is the last of this breed of authentic rock star, for he was an authentic bad guy who got over, and in so doing, forever changed the face of rock and roll.

Dee Dee was the archetypical fuck-up who's life was a living disaster. He was a male prostitute, a would-be mugger, a heroin dealer, an accomplice to armed robbery and a genius poet who was headed for prison or an early grave—but was side-tracked by rock & roll.

When I was 18 and doing Punk Magazine and hanging around the "Ramones Loft" at 6 East 2nd Street with Joey Ramone, trying to find money for beer instead of working, Dee Dee used to come by in the afternoon to write songs.

Dee Dee had lived at the "Ramones Loft," owned by the Ramones lighting and t-shirt guy, Arturo Vega, but was thrown out when his fights with his girlfriend, Connie, almost destroyed the place. I think the fight where they splattered the place with Arturo's paints was the final straw.

After he was thrown out, Dee Dee would show up with his well-worn repentant look, pick up the three-string folk guitar and huddle in the corner with Joey to thump out one of his

Surviving the Ramones

latest masterpieces. I would stand across the room astounded that his guy was actually capturing the complexity of our lives on the Bowery in the simplest rock & roll songs.

As a writer, Dee Dee always had a knack of distilling the most intricate ideas to their most basic forms without losing any of the context. Example:

> *"I dont wanna walk around with you,*
> *I don't wanna walk around with you,*
> *I don't wanna walk around with you,*
> *so why ya wanna walk around with me?"*

The entire story is there. Yeah, its blunt and simple, but if it's so easy, why didn't you do it?

Hearing Dee Dee's songs today, I'm still amazed at how emotionally and psychologically accurate they are. Musical snapshots of living degradation. Whenever I hear "Chinese Rocks," Dee Dee's anthem to copping heroin (that Johnny Thunders appropriated, though he had no part in writing) all the images of that time come flooding back to me. I can actually see Connie crying in the shower stall at Arturo's; Connie dragging Dee Dee out of the loft by his ear because he was about to fuck Eileen Polk in the bed by the windows; Dee Dee and Richard Hell taking the walk to Avenue C to cop; Dee Dee unable to sit down because Connie had stabbed him in the ass; Dee Dee pulling a knife on Johnny in the van because Johnny was calling Connie a pig . . . all those daily dramas of watching the Ramones go from a gang of incredible losers to an American institution.

I am forever grateful to have been able to witness, first hand, the mess of Dee Dee's life, and then watch how he

LOBOTOMY

transformed all that craziness, all that shit, into art. I hate people who use that term. They're usually no-talents pretentious pieces of shit who never had an original thought of their own. But I can use the word "artist" without any reservation when it comes to Dee Dee.

Because the guy really should have been a crime-spree newspaper headline instead of a voice and an attitude that inspired millions of kids to write songs, play music, join bands and re-invent themselves according to their own fantasies.

IN A time when the only voice around originates from the corporation instead of the heart, and kids are lining-up to conform to the mediocrity, then wake-up in the sludge of the brutal sameness with an automatic weapon in their hands, Dee Dee's life and work seems more valid than ever.

For Dee Dee taught us it was okay to feel like Charlie Starkweather or one of those kids with guns in Littleton, Colorado. But Dee Dee added, Why shoot your wad with just twenty minutes of fun, when you can scream out the depths of your desperation and keep the insanity going an entire lifetime?

Legs McNeil
Co-author of
Please Kill Me:
The Uncensored Oral
History of Punk.
North Hollywood, Calif.

Do you remember lying in bed

with the covers pulled up over your head

radio playing so no one can see?

—"Do You Remember Rock and Roll Radio?"

Introduction:

If there is a logic to this life, then I'd like to know what it is. I'm at the Chelsea Hotel in New York City again. I've taken a lot of drugs in this hotel. Now I'm going to get off drugs in this hotel. Strange, isn't it?

It's two weeks before my birthday. I am two weeks into withdrawal from methadone, which is the most addictive drug there is. This is going to be the hardest test for me, I can tell. It's going to be quite an experience. All the demons from my past are tormenting me.

They say that the Chelsea Hotel is haunted. I agree. A dragonfly is flying around in my room right now. A "she" dragon. Like Connie, one of my demons from a long time ago.

She flew into my room here seventeen years ago, didn't bother to knock; she just burst through the door yelling curses at me. Connie was very, very drunk. Eventually she passed out and slept it off; but before she did, she completely destroyed the place. She broke a champagne bottle on the radiator and tried to kill me with it—slashing at my neck with the sharp glass edges. Finally she exhausted herself and threw the broken bottle through the window, smashing it in the process. That was how Connie said good night: "Fuck you. It's over. Go to sleep." So I hit the sack.

In the morning we acted like everything was normal. We would get ourselves together the best we could, then go downstairs to the street and hail a cab to the Lower East Side, get out and go cop some dope from someone. This was 1974 or 1975. Connie was a go-go dancer. I was struggling in the Ramones. We were both dope addicts.

It's the beginning of a new era now and I am fed up with it all. I am going to fight back. I give the dragonfly a look that could kill, but she shrugs it off. She's in a frenzy now, flying at me from behind, then changing direction and flying straight at me. Trying to sucker me to look into the light. Fuck that. That ain't gonna happen.

Surviving the Ramones

    I am going to send every shitty memory I have of this hotel straight back to hell. I start a fire on the rug and come at her from behind. I set light to her head with another match, then watch her burn. Then I feel normal again. So I start to relax and stare at an unplugged fan, trying to will it to spin. Don't fuck with me.

    If you're experienced, I think you'll understand.

Dee Dee going up.
Barbara Zampini

Childhood

PART ONE

What I understand now is that I wasted a lot of effort

worrying about nothing. Probably because I felt like nothing.

My parents were horrible. Their lives were complete chaos

and they blamed it all on me.

My mother was a drunken nut job, prone to emotion-

al outbursts, where she would go spinning around the

apartment beating her fists in the air, or falling down and hammering the floor with them so as to let everyone know that she was tough and not to fuck with her. She called herself Tony, which is about as silly as me calling myself Dee Dee, when you think about it.

Besides having a mom who was a lot like Connie, my girlfriend when the Ramones started in the early '70s, I had a weak, selfish drunk for a father, who was somehow like Connie, too, and somehow like the person I became. Mom was a showgirl dancer at a cabaret called The Scala. My mother met my father after World War II in Berlin, where he was stationed with the U.S. army. My father just seemed to want to stay in Germany forever. He was still in the army in 1950. He thought he was German. He was just happier there.

They fell in love and got married. My father was thirty-eight years old and my mother was then just sweet seventeen. By the time I was born, my father had become a master sergeant, and every two years or so the family had to move from one shit German town to another.

I have seen pictures of my parents' wedding in Berlin, and they were a very nice-looking couple. My mother was very beautiful, I'll give her that, and my father was a handsome man. Both of them had those frozen, faraway, vacant stares, though. I guess living through the Second World War had fucked them up in the head. Mom had experienced the bomb raids that left Berlin a demolished shell. Dad had fought in the Battle of the Bulge and later Hamburger Hill in Korea.

■   ■   ■

MY MOTHER was born on a Sunday in 1931 in Berlin, in a hospital built by Frederick the Great. She seems to have had a very restrictive life, even though Berlin was a big city with plenty of violent crime. She was two years old when Hitler came into power in 1933. Those were terrible times. The communists and the Nazis were killing each other and beating each other up in the streets.

At school, it wasn't easy for her. Every day my mother and her classmates had to pay allegiance to the flag. Hold their arms up in the Nazi salute and sing "Deutschland Deutschland Über Alles" and "Die Faderland." "Deutschland Deutschland Über Alles" means "Germany, Germany over everything" and is rumored to have been written by Horst Wessel, a Berlin pimp, who later became a Nazi.

By 1936, the Olympics were staged in Berlin and the city was so clean it looked like the streets had been gone over with a toothbrush. By the time the Second World War started my mother was eight years old, and along with it came ration cards and block wardens. The Jewish people were forced to wear a yellow star on their clothes. Then came the *Krystallnacht*, the night all the Jews were attacked in their homes and in the streets. My mother remembers the screaming. She was a little girl, and not against anyone. She was scared.

Then came three years of bomb attacks. Everybody aged fourteen to eighty-four was ordered to defend Berlin. My mother was fourteen years old when the war ended. The city was full of dead bodies, everywhere. The river was full of dead bodies. My mother helped to bury them.

LOBOTOMY

There was an indoor swimming pool on an army base in Berlin that I discovered when I was about fourteen.

"Mom, it's great. Why don't you come swimming there with me?" I pleaded.

"Oh no, Douglas, I couldn't."

"Why not, Mom?" I asked.

"Because I remember that pool after the war. It was filled with the blood from the bodies of dead horses and dead people."

IN 1951, my father took my mother back to the States. They had me the next year in Fort Lee, Virginia. Not long after, my father was stationed in Korea. My mother and I followed him as far as Tokyo. For awhile, I was being raised by a Japanese woman named Kanui-san who carried me on her back. My only memory of Japan is of being taken to a Japanese Hansel and Gretel puppet show. I flipped out and they had to take me away; I was afraid of the witch.

For awhile we were stationed in Lynn, Massachusetts, where my sister, Beverly, was born. And that's when things started going bad. My father was constantly beating on me, yelling at me, and blaming me for everything. I started developing a really low self-esteem. It was dangerous to upset Beverly. She'd go tell mommy and daddy and they'd come after me. Or if they wanted to hurt each other they'd come after me. I was their punching bag.

Some of my earliest memories date back to the time when I was six years old and living in Munich, Germany, on another army base. I remember a lot of wild drunken fights between my parents. Once, late at night, I was woken up by noises coming from the living room. I got up out of bed to see what was going on, and peered down the hall to check out the situation.

My dad was sitting on top of my mother, smacking her around. They were both yelling and woke the whole building up. In the morning, everyone acted like everything was normal. It was weird to me, though. I couldn't really understand why my mom would be throwing all of our dishes out our fourth floor window. Or the times when I had to hold up Mom's head in the hope that Dad would pull over so she could throw up on the side of the road and not on me. My parents seemed so miserable that secretly I was hoping that Dad would just run our little German car right off the road, and kill our whole family.

Dee Dee and his Mother, Miami, 1997. *Barbara Zampini*

LOBOTOMY

MOM INTRODUCED me to rock'n'roll. She was a trouble-maker. She dressed cool and had a Bill Haley and the Comets EP, and that "I'm going to Kansas City" record. This was the late fifties—you couldn't ignore the teenagers in pegged black chinos and greasy hairdos, boppin' around the Munich American High School, which was right near the building where I lived.

I tried to go to school, but I failed the first grade, because I had no ability to concentrate. I was disturbed; I had anxiety problems; I had no self-esteem. I was embarrassed, because of the fighting in my family. And I had never been taught anything by an adult. I had absolutely no guidance. Everything was a mystery. I was totally helpless. I was worse than a child. I was a child child child. And I wasn't even as grown-up as the other kids my age. I would try to make up for my ignorance with physical enthusiasm, acting out, making funny noises. I had no idea I was even in school.

And then, when I was home, I was afraid. I didn't know what to do. I felt very awkward. I'd go home and my mom would tell me to hide. "Go somewhere else. Don't come here. He's here."

She was looking for someone to blame. And if she couldn't blame my father, she would blame me. I had no ability to study and learn and concentrate; to take my work home and have some peace and quiet; to feel dignified enough, or be able to ask someone a question.

I was developing all the traits of an unsatisfied person, which leads up to becoming an addict—a sense of unfulfillment, or chaos—a feeling that I needed more. I didn't know what it was that I needed, but I needed an escape or a strength. And I felt weak. I felt I was just floating on a cloud.

After failing first grade, I was too embarrassed to go back to school, except at lunchtime, when no one would see me. I would hide in the bushes and spy on the teenagers hanging out with their transistor radios. They wouldn't dance out there. Just diddy-bop around, stroll around, trying to look cool. This is how I could hear the music. I fell in love with rock'n'roll. It was exciting to me and seemed defiant. Like that song, "I'm Going to Kansas City."

My parents asked me what I wanted to be. They said, "You want to be in the military, right?"

I said, "*Ich mochte ein gamler.*" And that sort of means, I want to be a hobo.

They told me to shut up. In Germany kids are not supposed to speak. You can get an apartment in Germany with a dog but not with a kid.

I LIKED everything that seemed edgy. Like going to see the movie *The Mummy* with my mother, or going to see *The Ten Commandments* on my own. The film was six hours long, so they had this weird intermission where they opened up the exit doors so that everyone could go outside and smoke a cigarette or whatever. The contrast between the dark, safe, fantasy world in the movie theater and walking out into the blazing sunshine, where everybody could see each other, struck me as edgy. I worried about having my ticket stub to get back into the theater. *The Mummy* was crazier and sicker, but

LOBOTOMY

it was weird to see a complex film like *The Ten Commandments* on my own.

I remember thinking how thrilling it was when the cops brought Little Jimmy Preger, the local hood, into our building where we lived. He had passed out and they brought him upstairs on a stretcher. Jimmy had a "fuck you all for what you put me through" James-Dean–type look on his face. He didn't care any more. He was sixteen and doomed—and he knew it. I was seven years old, and my prospects seemed pretty bleak as well.

MY PARENTS continued to drink and drink. They'd rant and rave until they passed out, which really embarrassed me. There was never any peace and quiet. Even at five in the morning, they would be having it out. Once I wandered into the living room in my pyjamas to see what was going on. I was in a daze; Mom was going crazy again and I could see Dad holding her down and yelling "Call Miss Preger." Miss Preger was Jimmy's mom and lived in our building. My mom was yelling for me to call the police. Finally, someone else did and the cops came and arrested my mother. She locked me in the basement before they took her away.

My parents had some wild parties. One night, some of their friends jumped off the balcony for a goof. I don't know what happened to them after that. Dad couldn't be bothered to explain it to me. He was too busy getting drunk all over again. My mom too. She drank highballs made of Four Roses bourbon, Coke, and round ice cubes. They're pretty good, and make you feel like you're glowing.

Surviving the Ramones

It had gotten to the point where I had to avoid my father. It became too scary to come home. I spent most of my time wandering around the army base by myself. I had to live in a total fantasy world. The real world was too fucked up for me.

FOR A while in the early '60s, my family and I moved back to the States and lived in Atlanta, Georgia. My father got stationed there during the Cuban Missile Crisis, so we moved into a little apartment near the army base. My mother named it "Bugs Lane." They don't have that many bugs in Germany, but it seemed our whole new apartment was infested with them.

Bugs Lane was the first place I ever thought of committing suicide. The fighting was horrible; the alcoholism was really bad. My father used to come home at five in the morning and yell every single night: "LET ME IN! LET ME IN!"

I was about eleven years old and finally made a friend, a girl in my class. She liked that song by the Cavaliers—"Last Kiss." I finally talked to someone else about rock and roll music, the things we heard on the radio. I wish I could remember her name.

There was an active social life for the families of the soldiers on the Atlanta base, so we would go there to hang out a lot and that was fun. The soldiers and their wives were young, mostly in their teens and early twenties, and rock-'n'roll was blaring from the PX snack bar. This was where you could buy rock'n'roll records and transistor radios, Aqua Velva aftershave and Gold Cup socks. My sister and I would go to the enlisted men's club to do the twist.

LOBOTOMY

You could hear rock'n'roll at the swimming pool, too. It seemed to go along with the sun, the comic books, and the potato chips. On the weekends, they had dances that had the top twist bands. Mom, my sister Beverly, and I would always be there. Once, outside a fairground in a suburb in Atlanta, my father and I were walking past a trailer that had a stage built next to it. A tent was pitched out back behind the trailer, and there were girls in bikinis, dancing to a live rhythm and blues band. It was pretty sexy. You could go in the tent and watch the girls strip, but my dad and I just kept walking. I was glad to keep moving; my father would only have caused an embarrassing scene. He was a real ladies' man. He'd make me wait forever while he was chatting someone up. My sister and I would sit at a bar waiting for hours and hours. He was so cheap, he wouldn't even buy us a soda.

Once I ran out of a bar. I just said: "Fuck this!" And I ran out of there.

And he said, "Douglas! Douglas!"

And I turned around and said, "I'm gonna tell my mother!"

I don't know what good that would have done, but I said it anyway.

I HAVE one other strange memory of Bugs Lane. I saw something on TV there. It was a documentary of a mother at home with her three kids. They put on goggles and started sniffing glue.

Everything in America seemed more rebellious. I would go to the Minute Market and steal all the glue and model paint I could. Then I'd put the glue in a bag and sniff it. I actually

16

tried to make a few models, like a Fokker Triplane, but of course I had a defeatist attitude about everything and nothing ever worked. Once I tried to build a kayak with some boards I stole from a construction site.

I was always trying to build something. Another time I had seen a history book with Leonardo daVinci in it. I couldn't read but it showed him with the wings of a bird, flying. So I tried to build some wooden wings and fly off the roof, but luckily the neighbors caught me. I would have jumped off five stories. I was in a dreamland.

SOON, MY father was stationed back in Germany, when I was eleven or twelve. Pirmasens in Germany was a very violent, anything-goes kind of place. Everybody who lived there worked in one of the factories and a big cloud that smelled like a sewer hung over the place. If you lived there, you were sort of embarrassed to say so, because it was so rough. The population of Pirmasens was a mixture of wild American soldiers and their bored dependents, plus a lot of angry Germans. Germans and Americans don't get along too well.

Late at night, though, I would listen to the broadcasts from Radio Luxembourg, pirate radio stations from the English Channel. And they would play all these great songs by the Searchers, the Beatles, Paul Anka. "Put Your Head on My Shoulder." That's where the line in "Rock and Roll Radio" comes from: me, hiding under the covers, listening to Radio Luxembourg.

I didn't have many friends. I never have. Around my building, the kids would sit on the swings and spit at each other. If anyone brought marbles or toy soldiers to the playground, the other kids would surely lift them. We were mean and hateful and all had the same problems—fathers who drank themselves to death and beat up moms, and both parents taking it out on us. You tried to make the best of it. Being miserable seemed normal. There didn't seem to be any other way.

It was in Pirmasens that I had my first encounter with violence. It happened between me and this other kid called Krudd. Like me, Krudd had a German mother, and his father was stationed at the army base. He was a mess sergeant and spent most of his time planning meals for the troops—his free time he spent over at the enlisted men's club drinking and playing the slot machines. Krudd's mother, on the other hand, was a real German *hausfrau* type. She resembled what the Germans refer to as a *putzfrau*, which is a dirty, toothless hag that mops the stairways and is in one of those better-watch-your-step moods all the time. It's no wonder to me why Krudd was creepy. He could only be that way, especially since he was growing up in Pirmasens—he was guaranteed to be a loser.

Krudd was also on the minus-zero status socially at school. He was not popular. He was also smelly and overweight. He was just a creep, and treated accordingly by the other schoolkids. So Krudd and I had something in common. Neither of us were popular. Both of us were losers.

But Krudd had one thing going for him. He owned a Framus Tobacco Sunburst folk guitar, that somehow became very rock'n'roll when he picked it up in his beefy mugs. It was all about the mystery of owning a guitar. No one knew how to play guitars too well to rock'n'roll music then, so I gladly put up with watching Krudd show me a few things on the guitar. He showed me "The House of the Rising Sun" in open tuning, which I tried to practice. But soon the guitar novelty thing wore off—I have a short attention span. It was my fault and I could sense Krudd becoming increasingly agitated with me. Then at school one day, just before class started, I was rough-housing around with him, and out of nowhere, he hit me in the face with his fist, and it knocked me flat on my ass. I thought the fight was over; the teacher was getting real angry and wanted everyone to sit down so he could start our lessons. However, according to the local code, I had to meet Krudd later for a rematch after school.

I had stuck my neck unwillingly in the noose, and now I had to go to my own funeral. I felt sick, but there was nothing I could do. After school, I entered into the center of a ring of jeering, unsympathetic spectators. I knew then that I wasn't a fighter, but I had to do this. All my theatricality and fantasizing wouldn't help me out of this one. It was obvious that Krudd was going to beat the shit out of me. He was meaner and bigger than me, and also he had already sort of beat me up an hour before. I couldn't let that happen again, and since he was too tough an enemy for me to take apart with kicks and punches, I did what I had to do.

I pulled a blade on him. It was a pearl-handled switchblade with a razor-sharp four-inch blade. Weapons like knuckle-dusters and switchblades could be bought over the counter in Germany and everybody carried something. It was all part of it. This made Krudd back off. In a goofy sort of way, I was then able to take control of the situation. I bluffed my way out of it with a few thrusts and parries to the air, and by putting on that mean evil face that I know how to do. It was serious too—no one but my parents had ever hit me before. I was afraid of Krudd, so it was a good thing that he backed off. Needless to say, I lost his friendship too, but I never expected too much anyway, so what did I care?

PIRMASENS ALSO gave me my first introduction to morphine. One day I found a whole bunch of these morphine tubes hidden in a garbage dump behind a garage. Some poor young GI must have been planning to use them, no doubt having become familiar with scag back home in the States. It was around this time that Elvis Presley was stationed in Germany and it is rumored that he first started taking drugs in order to stay up during guard duty on those long, cold winter nights. The morphine came in khaki-colored toothpaste tubes with a big needle screwed onto the end. You jammed the needle into your thigh and squeezed the dope into the flesh. I was unfamiliar with drugs then—it looked too sick to do that to myself at that point in my life.

At first it might seem like a drag, because the morphine came with such a big needle, but a dope fiend would ignore that as a temporary inconvenience and do it anyway. The needles looked dangerous and threatening, but I took them over to the playground to show them off to a gang of the other kids. Nowadays, if you could get your hands on stuff like that, you would instantly be a very popular person with freaks lining up outside your door, but it was unheard of back then.

LOBOTOMY

Morphine is a heroin high in its more ancient form. A ticket to cloud nine where the kick is at its lushest. To get pharmaceutical ampulet styrets or phials of it is rare. Once, as I left the playground, I saw one of these styrets laying in the sand by the swings, so I brought a few of them home to show my dad. I was hoping it would make him proud of me for turning them in. When I got upstairs, he was there. He was acting like a caged animal and pacing back and forth in the small apartment. He seemed like he had a lot on his mind and was trying to hold back a lot of tension, but I took the risk and disturbed him.

"What are these, Dad?" I asked.

"Gimme those."

He smirked and snatched them out of my hands.

"Where did you get this stuff?" he asked me.

"Oh, I don't know."

"Well, get out of here!" he told me.

So I left. He was really angry. Dad really hated drugs.

SOMEHOW, EVEN at the age of twelve, I knew I was a loser. I couldn't see a future for myself. I thought the only thing I could hope to do was join the army. But, I didn't even make it for a week in the Boy Scouts. I was too afraid to ask my father any questions on anything, let alone ask him for permission to go on a camp-out.

Then I heard the Beatles for the first time. I got my first transistor radio, a Beatle haircut and a Beatle suit. It seems pretty crazy now, but this was 1963 and the Beatles were a big thing. I identified with these new rock'n'roll songs that were played on Radio Luxembourg, the pirate station that broadcast from the English Channel. They had Hubbly Bubbly commercials and played the Searchers, the Beatles, and the Dave Clark Five.

My sister, Beverly, and I also went to see movies like *Blue Hawaii* with Elvis Presley and *The Parent Trap* with Hayley Mills. When the Beatles' film *A Hard Day's Night* came out, all the kids in the theater fell in love. You could feel it. We all came out of there glowing.

Once, around this time, I was taking out the garbage and found a box of old *Playboy* magazines in the trash bin behind where I lived. I took them upstairs and looked them over. There was an article about a wrestler called Gorgeous George which caught my attention. He seemed to be a bit of a maniac. Somehow, my reaction to that article inspired the name Dee Dee to me. He didn't seem like anybody else. I liked that. Before the Beatles got real famous they had called themselves the Silver Beatles instead of just the Beatles. I guess everyone wanted to sound glamorous. It was in style then, and John Lennon called himself Johnny Silver. George was George Perkins and Paul was Paul Ramone. I thought it was pretty outrageous to change your name to a made-up one, but I liked the idea. I was lost in another fantasy, and changed from Douglas Colvin to Dee Dee Ramone.

Rebels were a lot cooler to me than squares. My parents seemed like a continual drag. I could never forgive them for what was going on at home. I don't know, maybe mom or dad would have been happier if I'd beat up my sister Beverly all

day and night, and started the morning with beer for breakfast, but by then I didn't care. I had my own scene.

I WAS hoping it would get better when we all moved back to
my mother's home town of Berlin, but it didn't. So what? By
now it didn't really matter to me. I had rock'n'roll and it gave
me a sense of my own identity.

I would go walking around the woods in Pirmasens for
hours and hours. Really going far, exploring. Looking for cas-
tles and bunkers. In Berlin I'd go into the bombed buildings,
into the basements of factories. The city was flat from the
war. But some kids made a mountain of rubble to go playing
and skiing. And I went up there with my sled and saw some
kids, a few years older than me, all dressed up, wearing
Beatle boots. They were making a fuss because they couldn't
get up the hill in their Beatle boots.

I tried not to go home as much as I could and I spent my
days shoplifting with my friend Robert at the big department
store, Ka De We, near Wittenberg Platz. We also tried to rip
off the antique shops around Nolendorff Platz for war relics
to sell to American GIs. Robert was American. His father
was there to write a book about Volkswagen.

We would try and sell the things we lifted by placing ads in
the PX or the community bulletin board. Then the CID would
come over to bust us, and they'd write us up on a typewriter.
They'd have to bring a typewriter into your house to write you
up. It was one of the last straws with my father. Before I had
just been a totally harmless idiot in a fantasy world. But now I
was busted by the CID like a serious criminal.

Surviving the Ramones

Robert and I spent hours in old bombed-out buildings and vacant shell-scarred lots, searching for more war relics to sell to antique shops. Our favorite hunting ground was Potzdammer Platz, where the big Banhoff had once been, and where Hitler's bunker had been too. Once, I found a Nazi helmet that someone had soldered a handle onto. Probably so that they could use it to cook potatoes in after the war was over.

They put up the Wall when we had previously lived in Berlin. Before the Wall had been erected I can remember Beverly, my mom and I taking the S Bahn into East Berlin to visit my grandparents. In those days, instead of a refrigerator, they had a closet called a "kool schrank." Somehow, the milk in Germany didn't seem to go rotten like the milk in America. Their apartment was heated by a coal fire and my mother's stepfather had a little coal yard which was watched over by a German shepherd named Greif. In the day time, Greif slept under the kitchen table but you couldn't pet him because he would bite.

It became forbidden for Americans to take the S Bahn. Robert and I used to ride the E Bahn under East Berlin, and when the subway train was in an East German station, it wouldn't stop; it would just race by and Robert and I would have our noses pressed against the window to make faces at the Vo Po's, who stood guard with Russian tommy-guns, like they did at Checkpoint Charlie.

Later on, when we moved to the American sector of Berlin, near Argentinisha Alle, I would walk Kessie, the fam-ily dachshund, in the mornings and pause for a minute to wave at the tanks clanking down Argentinisha Alle to the Grune A Wald. Then, at four o'clock the tanks would clank back up to the Argentinisha Alle to the motor pool. All the kids in the neighborhood would cheer them, and then it was time to go home for dinner.

No one was ever home at my house. Mom was normally with Beverly at the ballet school where my sister was taking dancing lessons. Dad was nowhere to be seen. So I was there, alone with Kessie. I would listen to the rock'n'roll on the Armed Forces radio shows, stuff like "Dang Me" by Roger Miller. Or I would go to the PX snack bar, where I could get a cheeseburger and a chocolate milkshake. I would also sit up in my room alone and read *16* and *Hit Parade* magazines about groups like the Monkees, Paul Revere and The Raiders, and also Dino, Desi, and Billy. I would also try to play my Italian electric guitar which I had bought at the Music Haus Am Zoo near Ausburger Platz. I went there every day and stood outside and looked at the guitars in the window. The one I liked most was a green Sunburst Echo, with three white pick-ups and a tremolo arm.

The bands in Berlin played the Liverpool Hoop and the Berlin American High School. They would set up their Selmer PA columns and their Vox amplifiers and run through the hits of the day, like "Working in A Coal Mine," "The Midnight Hour," and "Gloria" by the Shadows of the Night. These bands were amazing. The best were the Hound Dogs, the Restless Sect, and especially the Boots.

By then I'd begun to take dope. There were lots of dealers around the Braunhoff Am Zoo area. They would fill the

hypodermic needles from big plastic bottles of liquid morphine. The German dope was strange, but it was fun. It felt
like you were getting an electric shock when you shot it up.
Then you went completely numb. I would have done it more
often than I did, maybe three times a month, but I was too
afraid of my father. Of course, later, when I moved to New
York, I got more serious about drugs.

Clothes were also high on my must-have list. Levi's jackets
were in suede, yellow, or cranberry. Hush Puppies came in
pale green or baby blue corduroy. You picked up ideas of what
to wear from many of the bands that played in Berlin around
that time. I thought the Rolling Stones were the most edgy
dressers. It was a great time for music and I saw the Troggs,
the Kinks, the Small Faces, the Hollies, the Beach Boys, the
Rolling Stones, The Who, and the Walker Brothers.

Then one day I woke up and Berlin was plastered with
pictures of Jimi Hendrix. He had an Afro, was biting his
teeth together, and playing the fuck out of a Fender
Stratocaster that he was shaking behind his head.

MY MOTHER was planning an escape. She was living her
life over through my sister, Beverly—trying to get Beverly to
accomplish what she wanted to accomplish and didn't. My
mother had wanted to be a ballet dancer, too.

My sister Beverly had gotten accepted into Julliard to
study with Balanchine, and my mother told me we were
going to go to New York. I was so happy. I had read in *Hit
Parade* magazine about the scenes in America. They had all
the clubs listed in New York.

LOBOTOMY

Everything was packed and divided. My parents had gotten a divorce. But they didn't really discuss it with me. It was always so mysterious, 'cause you never really knew where they were, anyway.

ABOUT TWO days before we left, my dad started really yelling and acting out—over thirty-five cents.

He knew we were leaving but he never discussed it with me. I had had it. I was ready to stab him. I was squaring off, palming my blade behind my back. I was ready to get him back once and for all.

He was a real man's man. All my friend's fathers were that. I used to go to my friends' house, and they'd go in their fathers' drawer and show me their knucks.

Then I stopped and asked myself, *Well, how can I kill this man?* And I just kinda fizzled out and said: *I can't. He'll just put me on the pavement 1, 2, 3.*

Two days later, we took a plane.

My father had gotten out of control once too often and we had to run for our lives.

A couple of weeks after leaving Berlin I was

living in Forest Hills, Queens, New York. It was a good idea

to get out of Berlin when we did. Having left my father, I

thought things would get better, but they just got stranger.

Somehow, I just couldn't relate to my new neighborhood.

At least in Berlin you didn't have to be on alert all the time.

LOBOTOMY

Forest Hills is one of those neighborhoods which is a subway ride to and from Manhattan—it's about twenty minutes on the F train and G local to 8th Street and Sixth Avenue. It is a nicely groomed neighborhood with lots of Coupe deVilles and Lincolns parked on the street. All the buildings are the same redbrick color and chewing-gum-colored sidewalks snake through the area. There are little fringes of grass hugging the buildings where dogs go to the bathroom. In the mornings, the janitors would burn the trash in incinerators and a thick gray smoke would pour out of the chimneys. I loved it in the morning. As soon as I would hit the sidewalk, I would kind of catch myself and then peer through the morning confusion, on alert.

Kessie, our dog, whom we had brought with us from Berlin, would scamper out of the lobby, down the stairs to the street, her nails clicking behind her. I would stand lookout for her. Then, Kessie would change from the ready to the action position, squirt the sidewalk, and bolt back into the building while I was watching out for the police. They were so fussy. If you were caught letting your dog run off the leash, you could get a summons. The cops would ride around on motor scooters in the morning looking for trouble—blue knights in plastic armor. They were forever giving out parking tickets and looking out for kids who didn't go to school.

Some of the kids I met were very well-off. I couldn't compete with them, and I didn't feel like them. Not because they were nasty to me; it was my own problem. I just didn't fit in.

I STARTED drifting into Manhattan, taking the subway to the Village. The first time I took it to the city, I got off at

Surviving the Ramones

Roosevelt Avenue and had to ask someone on the platform next to me—"How do you get to Greenwich Village?" I felt so foolish, but I was headed in the right direction. It was easy. I just had to step into the F train.

It was a cool time in New York. I kind of knew where to go from the listings in *Hit Parade*. I went to check out the Night Owl, but it wasn't a rock club any more—they just sold Day-Glo posters. So, I went over to the Café Wha which was completely splashed in Day-Glo paint. There you could see live bands like the Raves, Cherry People, and Kangro.

Although drugs were becoming a big influence on youth culture, they were still sort of a mystery. The message in the Village was "Turn on, tune in, and drop out," but at first I didn't know where to get any drugs. The Café Wha was where Jimi Hendrix had pioneered psychedelic music, but the atmosphere in there was so soothing that, when a good band was on, I felt completely like I didn't need anything else.

A month after we moved to Forest Hills, I took my first tab of acid. I met my new friend Egg on Queens Boulevard, and we each took a Blue Flat. Our other friends asked us if we had done it before, and we said "Yeah, sure." It was a beautiful trip and when I came home the next morning, even my mother seemed to be in a good mood, but she struck first.

"Douglas, you seem to be in a good mood. Why are you so cheerful this morning. What's up with you?"

"Oh, I don't know, Mom," I said. Then I blurted out, "Oh, I just took some LSD last night with my friend Egg, and I am still tripping. I feel wonderful. Even the cereal looks beautiful. I wonder what's in those cornflakes?"

LOBOTOMY

"Well," she said, "let's listen to the new Jimi Hendrix album, Doug. It's called *Are You Experienced?* So I finished my breakfast and rolled a joint. I didn't bother to get any sleep. I had to be at Daitch Shopwell, the supermarket on 108th Street where I had just got a job, in a couple of hours, so I just sat there in a daze until my mom left for work. All I could think of was getting some dope from my friends at work to calm me down from the acid.

LSD was fun. I did it hundreds of times, and I don't think I ever had any bad trips, but it really wasn't my thing. It was heroin that would get me through the day. Early on I could sense the big problem with narcotics was that they tended to lead to crime. If you use heroin, you catch a habit and end up a slave to the drug. Sooner or later you start to lead a double life and lie for drugs and dollars until you eventually become consumed by the whole experience and take on a new identity as a criminal misfit. Once heroin gets its claws into you, you'll end up doing anything, legal or otherwise, to get a fix.

I have such a weak, criminal mentality, that my new criminal identity consisted mainly of making associates with the local hoods in the area, like my friend Jeff, who was already doing armed robberies and breaking and entering with this other guy Ricky and his friends. Jeff was a big kid for his age, and strong. I never saw him rob anyone but he used to come to the supermarket and show us the money he'd stolen. Then he would put some steaks under his jacket and just walk out. You couldn't argue with him, but he was a nice guy. Later on, he found Jesus while on acid.

After this, Jeff decided he didn't want to do any more robberies, and especially not with Ricky's gang of friends. But, Ricky said that Jeff was too involved and it was too much of a risk to let him out of it. So, what they did was walk Jeff over the bridge into Flushing Meadows Park and killed him. They assaulted him, stabbing him over and over again, but somehow he refused to die. Finally, everyone left, Jeff was lying on the grass, bleeding to death, and that was it. I guess dying alone was the only peace he'd ever get. It didn't seem like he deserved to die like that.

Forest Hills was a pretty open-minded neighborhood, but heroin was more of a city thing, so I would cop it in Manhattan in the fleabag areas, and sometimes at the fountain in Central Park. I would buy a half load from my dealer in the park every day for twenty-four dollars. This was when the dope in America was coming into the U.S. from France. It came in glassine envelopes and was cut with quinine. I always felt like that's when we were getting the real stuff. After that, the heroin was never the same. It was strong and made you scratch yourself and nod out. A half load of dope was fifteen two-dollar bags. If I sold them, three were mine. I could get three dollars a bag for them in Queens, so I always sold some to my friends. When I went back to Forest Hills, I was making out pretty good.

My sister Beverly wasn't doing so hot. Within a year of our moving there, she got married and stopped dancing with Balanchine. That started another big row between her and my mother and flipped everybody out.

LOBOTOMY

I COULD already see America changing and I had only been there a few months. There was a lot of funky stuff going on. It was getting looser. In Central Park they started getting guys there on the weekend pushing supermarket carts around, stacked with beer cans on ice. You could get beer. Cold beer. Right in the park. Cop it like dope. In the liquor stores you could start buying wine that tasted like pop, so that kids could drink it.

Things were getting more outlaw. You could see street gangs like The Savage Nomads starting up in the suburbs, where they had not been seen before. Now they were coming on strong. One day the Nomads came into the park to fight another gang from the South Bronx. These guys were violent. They were saying one thing to everybody—Fuck You. Another time, I saw some of them hassle a dope dealer sitting by the band shell fountain. They whacked him with pool cues pretty bad. If that wasn't bad enough they also started whacking his Doberman.

I saw a tattoo of Jesus on a guy's shoulder during that summer. I was about sixteen or seventeen years old and didn't have any tattoos yet. In 1969 a tattoo like that was really weird. It was as outlaw as you could get. The ultimate way of saying "don't fuck with me." Later, I got that same tattoo as my own little way of saying I was sick of having to conform to everything, just because the Ramones had a look. When I went for therapy, it was something which I almost came to blows about with my psychiatrist, Doctor Jagger. I had to convince him to get it. What a laugh! I was a full-grown adult, and yet I was struggling to get his permission over something so stupid. I still think that's crazy.

1969 WAS the year of the summer of hate. For me, it wasn't about going to see Jefferson Airplane at the Central Park band shell and taking LSD. It was about sitting on a park bench drinking wine and snorting deuce bags of heroin.

I wonder if there wasn't some systematic plan from somewhere to fuck up people in America. Letting dope into the country on purpose to fuck up fools like me, who they saw as the burdens of society. It was well known that the CIA was on the side of the opium warlords, so they wouldn't sell out to the Chinese Communists and go red. And also because it's so profitable—drugs are money. And where did those orange tang methadone biscuits come from? Was it just part of the deal? It's a big letdown to be sixteen years old and already know that nothing's going to change.

I thought America was the land of equal opportunity, but I didn't have the opportunities that the other kids in Forest Hills had. We were all fucked up, but my situation was even worse.

I didn't go to school but I was signed in. For awhile, they really did me a favor keeping me signed on, so I wouldn't have to go in the draft. That was my only real break from Forest Hills High School.

I was working in a supermarket and dealing drugs, trying to save up enough money to buy a car.

When my mother found out I wanted a car she was happy. She thought I would drive her to Rockaway Beach in the summer or something, so she suggested that I write my

LOBOTOMY

father a letter and ask him for the money. I did, and he wrote me back a "fuck you" letter. That was the end between him and me. He was a useless bastard and I hated him, but I don't know where I was coming from asking him to buy me a car. Christ, that was stupid. My mother was stupid to suggest it.

I had a bad reaction to his letter. He didn't know how to be a father or take care of anybody. He didn't care and he didn't love me. I was what ruined both of their lives; maybe they could have had more fun without me. As usual, I was alone, on the street, and that was that.

When I was sixteen, I met a girl named Linda at

Harlow's discotheque. She was older, about twenty-two,

Italian, really nice, really pretty. And she was going to college,

uptown on 68th Street.

I didn't feel like I had a home. But Linda took good care

of me and I loved her.

LOBOTOMY

Unfortunately, Linda's mother didn't want me around. And I can't blame her now. Her mother was being protective of her. She put a lot of money into the girl. They were really poor. I don't think she had a father. And she was going to college. And, what was she doing with me, anyway? I was a kid.

Linda broke up with me and broke my heart. My dreams of making music weren't amounting to anything. My prospects were getting bleaker and bleaker.

If I had been perfect, my mother might not have minded me moving back home. But, by then, the sad truth was, no matter what my parents were, I was no better. A lot of times I wouldn't come home because I was too high

I wrote my mom a note: *I'm gonna go to California*. I took my bass over to the pawnshop and pawned it for $65. And with the money I took a cab somewhere to New Jersey—to Route 80—and then I started hitchhiking to California.

I was sleeping on the side of the road by a tree in Flint, Michigan when I got picked up by some guys. It didn't take too long to figure out they were serious criminals, doing robberies and stuff. They were the real deal, and I was out of their league.

I rode with them to Indiana. They were playing bad things in the car, driving real slow up and down the highway. They had a flexible saw, and they were planning to decapitate the next person they met.

Lucky for me the cops pulled us over and busted us in South Bend. They separated us; somehow they knew I wasn't with them even though I was carrying a big bowie knife. They threw me in jail. I was in the bullpen in the daytime and a four-man cell at night. Three weeks later, they let me out. I hopped on a bus to Chicago and got back on the highway, to hitchhike to California.

In Texas, this one guy in a Corvette picked me up. He was wearing a black cowboy outfit. And then, he pulled off to the side of the road all of a sudden. He took out a rifle and starting shooting at birds. He asked me if I wanted to take a couple of shots. He told me he would catch crayfish and cook them up in his hubcap. We went to his mom's house for something to eat, and he had alligators in his backyard. Then he drove me back to the highway.

Finally, I got a really long ride from someone who lived in California. They dropped me off at Newport Beach, and I slept on the beach at night. The next day, a service guy and his friend picked me up, and they had mescaline. I took it and they dropped me off on the Sunset Strip, right by the Whisky a GoGo.

I didn't like L.A. I was alone, and it was the end of it all. The vibe was bad there. It was violent on the Strip. The street people were taking serious dope, Tuinols and M & M's which are little miniature Tuinols.

I hitchhiked down to Route 1 and then took Route 1 to Big Sur. I lived in Pfeiffer Park for a long time, alone in the woods on LSD. I went to The Gorge, where there's a stream between two mountains. There were all kinds of people in the woods—freaks—who'd ask you if you wanted something to eat.

I hitchhiked back to Culver City and got a job in a bakery as a maintenance man at night. I had to go in at midnight

LOBOTOMY

and clean big trash cans with a hose. Meanwhile, I was living in the Washington Hotel on Washington Boulevard, getting into crime, driving around with robbers looking for people to mug. The only people I associated with were misfits and crooks. Everybody was bad there. You couldn't bring any food or beer into the place without someone knocking on your door trying to hustle you. "You got an extra beer?"

The whole lifestyle was scary, and it's scarier to me now because I feel like I didn't have much of a criminal mentality. To this day, I don't know how I avoided more serious consequences.

I do think that what saved me was that I had another interest, which was music. I still had fantasies about being in a band. When I was in Culver City, the MGM studios were closing. I would go there for the auctions. They were selling all the costumes from *Ben Hur* and stuff like that. I started checking out thrift shops in the neighborhood. And I'd always find those little suitcase boxes of 45's and go through them. I was getting all the great songs: "Last Kiss" and Jimmy James and the Fireballs and "Sugar Shack." I didn't have a guitar but I had a little record player in my hotel and I'd listen to all these records that nobody cared about anymore.

Later, I'd discover that Mick Jones and Joe Strummer of The Clash and Steve Jones of the Sex Pistols and I all listened to the same twenty-five long-forgotten songs, songs like "Sha La La La Lee" by the Small Faces. And it was mostly because they had power chords in the songs instead of a guitar break. Steve Marriot of the Small Faces would shake his guitar around and just let it *hummm*. When I was a little boy I had a Steve Marriot haircut, Steve Marriot shoes, and Steve Marriot pants. I was always dreaming of having a Steve Marriot guitar.

Before long I was back in jail. I had stolen a car and taken a bunch of M & M's and wrecked the car on the side of the road in Malibu. It was a really nice jail. And they let me go! For no reason, they just let me free! I've always been sure that someone has been watching over me.

I was wearing a suede fringe jacket that my friend had given to me when he committed suicide. He wrote it in his suicide note. I went walking that night, up by the Whisky and then down the Strip. Some guy started following me and saying, "Hey, let me try on your jacket, let me try it on." They were trying to take this jacket from me, and they got it, and left me with a black eye. I was getting depressed. The facts of adult life were hitting me. I was totally in this low-life criminal crap and I wanted to play music. But I had no idea how I could ever play. I was so used to having my mother as some kind of stability in Forest Hills, even though she threw my guitar out the window and broke all my records.

I moved in with a bunch of freaks in this house in Hollywood. It was completely nuts. Everybody was taking STP and pills and trying to look like Keith Richards but nobody was playing music.

I tried to hitchhike home, but I ended up in Vernal, Utah and I had to turn back; back to Los Angeles through Las Vegas. There were these anti-hitchhiker people there that would drive by and throw things like apples at you from their trucks.

LOBOTOMY

I can't remember leaving LA again and hitchhiking east, but somehow I ended up at my grandma's house in Missouri. She was very religious. Sometimes, she would sleep so quiet in her chair, I didn't know if she was dead. After she made me flush my pot down the toilet I decided it was time to head back home to Forest Hills.

There I was, back in Queens. I was a high-school dropout, which was kind of lower class for Forest Hills. The key to survival seemed to be a college education, but I had already graduated to my role in life—that of social deviant. There wasn't much I could do about it. I am ok with it now, but back then I wanted to climb up the ladder to success. At least a little bit.

So, after scanning the *New York Times* for a few weeks, I finally accepted a job in an insurance company, Employers Insurance of Warsaw, or something horrible like that. I liked working there, delivering the mail in the office every day.

I didn't know where I was headed, but it was a start.

Blitzkrieg Bop!

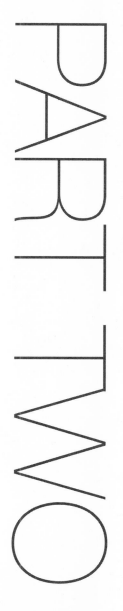

PART TWO

By the early seventies, I wasn't bothering with Forest

Hills that' much any more, or my old haunts like the Café

Wha or the Fillmore East. The scene had moved to mid-

town Manhattan and the Upper West Side. Disco music

was all the rage, and with it came the glitter clothes. The big

thing then was the "Super Nature" thing, like Shaft and

LOBOTOMY

Superfly. The cool clubs were the Sanctuary, Tamberlane and Superstar. These were Harvey Wallbanger and Quaalude clubs—places to hang out until the small hours.

Before I ever was a rock star with the Ramones, I was one of the cool glitter people of New York. People thought I was a rock star. Johnny too. They would stop Johnny in the bathroom at Alice Cooper concerts and ask him when he was gonna go on.

I was going out at night and going to the mailroom during the daytime. I would go to work with coffee and a buttered roll from Chock Full o' Nuts, a copy of the *Post* and a bunch of loose joints to sell to the other guys in the mailroom. Sometimes I would skinpop milky-white heroin to cope with the pressure. Then I started mainlining it. The track marks sort of tattoo you, no matter if you've planned it or not. To get the money for my little dope habit, I would sometimes empty the change box in the soda machine at work and keep the cash. Or I'd take the subway instead of a cab when doing a delivery for my job. I was also selling dope to my friends. I could feel myself transcending into a sort of negative Jesus. Nobody wanted to see me around in Forest Hills any more. That was ok. They would all pester me for dope sooner or later.

We were into "Shaft," Bowie, T Rex, and "Rock the Boat." I was recreating what I only dreamed about in Germany: the life of a Carnaby Street mod, which basically means living at home, working as a clerk, and putting all your money into style. I was lucky because there was a valid new youth culture to go along with my dream.

Surviving the Ramones

What I found out was that girls liked me. And I became very manipulative, living off of a lot of women, women like Sarah Rico who was a secretary at the insurance company. She was a twenty-eight-year-old sexpot who walked into the mailroom in a miniskirt to ask me if I would go out with her little sister. Then I started seeing her and everybody in the office just dropped dead. It was like I had won tickets to the baseball series. She took care of me, tried to steer me in the right direction.

John liked Gerri Miller, the go-go dancer Andy Warhol star. She was dancing at the Metropole and we'd go spy on her. She would hit people on the street with her purse and always cause a ruckus.

Instead of hanging out in the parks around Queens at night, I was becoming a night owl around New York. Places around 48th and Lexington or around Central Park West like the Forbidden Fruit, a late-night juice bar for young deviants—somewhere hip where you wouldn't expect it. Girls that went there usually worked at massage parlors and took care of businessmen during their lunch hours or when they got out of work at five. These girls would go to the Fruit to celebrate with their pimps. The club would be filled with Spanish and Italian kids doing the Hustle and the Bump. All the boys that went there tried to look cool and were always looking for trouble.

There were two big street fights outside the club during the few short months it existed. As the club was closing, people would start to mingle outside, hanging out on the sidewalk. The guys would break off car antennas and whip out

LOBOTOMY

007 knives—always a favorite knife in New York. Everyone was all dressed up in platform shoes and glitter-disco outfits, making it even more theatrical. The action was so fast that it was quite breathtaking. One gang would run down the street attacking the guys on the other side. Then that side would retaliate scattering their opponents. It would happen in the street, between the parked cars, not on the sidewalk, and everyone would stuff themselves into this small space. You couldn't tell what was going to happen, because it was so fast and it was so crowded. When it cleared, there was always someone left lying on the pavement.

Another time outside the Fruit, I saw this big, loud-mouthed creep get stabbed. The guy who stabbed him didn't make any motions to fight or anything like that. He just stabbed the creep and ran. The creep just lay there moaning—"He stabbed me as I was getting out of there!"

It would have been nice if you could have walked out of the Fruit at closing time, straight past all the other creeps and into a waiting hearse. Then you could lay down in a coffin, close the lid, and be driven off somewhere. Better than trying to leg it to the 59th Street Bridge to catch the bus to Rego Park with some girl from Flushing that's just taken her shoes off and thrown them away. She's real out of it on Quaaludes, and can't walk very well. She's too much of a burden for me. It's just too messy and I am not in the best of shape myself. So, as the crowd from the Fruit fades, so do I. As I am walking away, I turn around to see what she is doing, and she flashes me the finger and a "Fuck you, Jack!" frown. She's not going anywhere—I think to myself that it's better if

Surviving the Ramones

I leave her to her own devices. I am going back to Queens and that's not easy after a Friday night at the Fruit.

Thank God it's Saturday, I think to myself again. As I walk past Jumping Jack Flash, I give it the finger. It pisses me off because it's the store where I bought my cool white platform shoes with stacked heels, but they're killing me. I want to go home.

The bus lets me off on Queens Boulevard, near Rego Park, which is a bitch. I don't even want to think about the walk back to my mother's apartment from the bus stop. She lives on 66th Road, near the Hermits House. It's a long walk and I am dressed up in the shoes, satin pants, and glitter top. My feet are sore and I am tired. Just another creep in the smoggy city, trying not to acknowledge the new day. The sun doesn't feel warm. It's not innocent like the sun in upstate New York, in the country, on a Saturday morning.

Instead, this sun comes up opaque, trying not to be seen. It's more comfortable in the dark, lurking near subways and below the buildings that tower above Manhattan. It gives me that unfocused feeling like how I feel about modern technology. I have the long walk to nowhere to look forward to. It's ok. It doesn't phase me. People like myself aren't supposed to be going anywhere. If there's a bit of paranoia in the air, then that's fine. How else could it be? I didn't exactly want to go home. Not when I was caught short with no dope, no money, and going into withdrawal.

THEN MY mother yelling at me as soon as I walk into the apartment, and there's me, shaking with cold even though it's

49

summer, sick because I need some heroin, and in no mood for any bullshit from anyone, least of all from her.

Mom doesn't seem to be aware that this might become a bad scene. She's so used to these types of dramas that she reacts to it in the typical way she's always seen it done. She picks up a pot of old spaghetti off the stove and flings it at my head, splattering the wall with rotten meat sauce.

"Cut it out, you creep!" I shouted at her. "That could have been my brain splattered on the wall instead of spaghetti."

That was all the excuse she needed to completely freak.

"You bastard! Coming home on dope! I'm going to kill you!"

She picked up my treasured Echo guitar and held it over her head in the battle-axe position, and then got right down to serious business, chopping up the furniture, everything, the lamps, the records, the record player.

The whole time she's doing this demolition job on the apartment, she's yelling at me "I hate you! I hate you! I'm going to kill you!" Then she started shouting "You're just like your father!" That really pissed me off.

But I wasn't afraid of her any more, especially since my father was still in Berlin. So I decided to go at her like Dad would, and for the first time I yelled and cursed her back.

"You old German hag! Get the fuck out of here, you whore cunt!"

I thought she was going to shit herself. She looked really frightened and left. She ran right out the door. I had never seen her make a decision so quickly before. Never. Even though it was her apartment, for once I think she did the right thing. I wasn't going to take her abuse and yelling any more, so I gave her a taste of her own medicine. I wasn't an innocent, defenseless child any more, so she was really risking it. I never asked her for anything, she was too crazy. By then I was a vicious creep with a lot of hate in me. I guess my mother realized that, so she ran for her life. I wish I'd punched her in the face. I picked up the Echo and trashed the rest of her apartment instead. Then I threw the broken guitar through the living room window, slammed the door off the hinges and left. What else could I do? Walk her over the bridge to Flushing Meadow Park? Still, if I got angry with someone, I would go for the throat. I thought that was normal. Why do you think I ended up in the Ramones, who were described as a barrage of white hate?

People who join a band like the Ramones don't

come from stable backgrounds, because it's not that civi-

lized an art form. Punk rock comes from angry kids who feel

like being creative. I guess that's why members of the

Ramones were known to throw TV sets from the roofs of

apartment buildings at people below on the street. We had

a special hatred for old ladies pushing their carts full of groceries home from the supermarket. In Forest Hills, you would find used TV sets on the sidewalk every day, when the janitors in the area put the trash out on the street to get picked up in the morning. It was great. When those TVs hit the street, the tubes exploded on the concrete and they scared the shit out of people. It was something to do.

When you're sixteen years old, angry and bored, you have to be very creative to stir up some excitement. Like those dried up old Christmas trees the janitors would put in the basements after the holidays were over. The kids in my neighborhood would sneak down there and set them on fire. Then they would run back out to the street and stand there and laugh.

By then I had become a manic-depressive. I was hopeless. I could only laugh at someone else's expense and I thrived on negativity. I can see now how it was only natural that I would gravitate toward Tommy, Joey, and Johnny Ramone. They were the obvious creeps of the neighborhood. All their friends had to be creeps. No one would have ever pegged any of us as candidates for any kind of success in life. But that's how it goes.

The Ramones were the elite of the rebel class in Queens during the late sixties and early seventies. Definitely not high school student, college material types. Instead of school and homework, we were into goofing off and fantasy-making. All of us were a bunch of ill-mannered lowlifes. We thought cripples were funny because you could goof off on them— like it was lucky to rub a midget's head, especially if the midget was bald. I was off-the-wall enough to see some kind of logic in those kinds of superstitions.

If I had to run with anyone in Forest Hills, then it had to be with an off-the-wall type or worse. When I first met Johnny Ramone, it was at the top of the hill on 66th Road, near the Hermit's House. John was delivering dry cleaning from the cleaners where he worked. That was his full-time gig. Later he worked as a construction worker at 1633 Broadway, in the same building where I worked as a mail clerk. John's hair was real long then. Down to his waist, like Mark Farner from Grand Funk Railroad. He had on tie-dyed jeans and a tie-dyed headband and those same cheap Keds that he still wore even when our band got famous and we had money.

John was always very friendly to me and eventually we started talking about guitars and amplifiers and stuff like that. I started telling him a fantastic story about the equipment that I owned, probably like the one Bill Wyman must have told Mick Jagger and Keith Richards to get into the Rolling Stones. I said I had a twin Sound City stack and a plush amp with a two eighteens cab. Actually I played my Hoffner Beatle bass through a friend of mine's amp. It was a real old Ampeg, with one eighteen-inch speaker. It's hard to describe that amp. It was sort of embarrassing. No one knew how good they sounded then, because they looked so weird. I blew up my Vox Pacefinder or Escort or whatever they were called, a ten-watt amp with an eight-inch speaker. I kept the Vox at my mom's apartment, but it was ruined from using it with a boss tone to dirty up the sound.

LOBOTOMY

The Who had just played Central Park and John and I liked them then. Pete Townshend had smashed up all these Sound City amps. Later, Townshend got those cool Sunn amps like the Stooges used.

John is a very strong-willed person. He was one of the first friends I made when I moved to America and our friendship was based on music. When I first told John that the Stooges were my favorite group, he said he liked them also. I couldn't believe it. Someone else in Forest Hills liked the Stooges besides me. It was like a miracle. To me, the Stooges were the most real rock'n'roll band around. They were the best. The original Stooges, with Iggy, Ron and Scott Asheton, and Dave Alexander. They were very, very creepy. Creepy is the best description for them. They were the kings of the creeps.

John was always way ahead of his time. He wasn't biased about music, he'd give anything a chance. But he had his tastes. He liked outrageous, loud, raunchy rock music. He was older than us and seemed to know a lot of other things too. He would tell us sick stories, trying to hip us up and we wouldn't have a clue. He would tell us stuff like how he'd been to see the Yardbirds at the Anderson Theater and the first Rolling Stones concert at the Academy of Music. He'd thrown rocks at the Beatles when they played Shea Stadium. John also liked Ted Nugent, the MC5 and Black Sabbath. He had seen Black Sabbath's first show in New York at Steve Paul Scene.

We both loved Jimi Hendrix. John saw him play at the Café Wha back in 1966 or 1967. He said it was quite an experience. Jimi had apparently played a guitar that was completely broken off at one end of it—it didn't phase him one bit. When he broke a string, he didn't stop playing. A Stratocaster is hard to re-string anyway, but Hendrix could put a new string on his guitar while still playing. Finally, he threw the Strat over his head into the Fender twin, and it snapped in two. Then he cooed into the mike that everyone should go over to Central Park tomorrow to see him play. He was opening up for the Young Rascals, and he told everybody he was doing the gig to get a new guitar.

We used to check out the guitars on 48th Street together. Johnny Ramone never broke a guitar. He couldn't be bothered. He found one he liked and always played the same one. A Mosrite like the Stooges used. Except for the strobe tuners, Johnny Ramone never spoiled himself. He made the most with what he had. That's what I liked about him then. Still, it's sort of strange to play sick music on a Mosrite which is really supposed to be a surf guitar. Somehow they're alright to use with fuzz tones and stuff. They also go very well with bowl haircuts.

John was always doing things his own way. He had a big guitar amp speaker, and a tiny Sony tape recorder, and somehow that was his stereo. Richie Stern and him had a lot of tapes—they would sneak cassette players into concerts and make tapes of bands. They'd bootleg things for us, like if the MC5 were playing, or the Stooges.

Richie lived in Lefrak City. He was a very special person, a big Stooges fan—a very crazy supermarket clerk dope-fiend type. He would play Stooges tapes for us and do Iggy impersonations by the light of the glowing TV set. Then he would

LOBOTOMY

sing things back to the tape. I'd sit there on the floor and watch him with amazement. Richie was a weirdo and originally we wanted to have him play bass in the Ramones. We had one rehearsal with him, but he refused to join because by then he had started working at OTB. He had put $3,500 in the bank in seven months. Not bad for an eighteen-year-old creep from Lefrak City.

Seeing Joey Ramone in Forest Hills then was a

weird sight. Joey was very tall, and had a red Afro hairstyle,

modeled after Jimi Hendrix's. It was called the Explosion

and was the sort of haircut you could get at Paul

McGregors' in the East Village. Joey looked like a druggy.

He could usually be seen wearing a yellow suede fringed

jacket from Paul Sargent's, cranberry corduroy trousers from The Naked Grape, moccasins instead of sneakers, and those freaky round tinted glasses that he still wears today.

Joey was my drinking partner. We would buy a bottle of wine, put it in a paper bag, and sit on a stoop drinking it. My mother really liked him, which is strange. She would get so excited if he ever came over to see if I was home. She would always say to me, "Oh, Joey came by," but she wouldn't tell me if anybody else came by. And she would always be asking me questions about him. I told her I didn't know myself. Later I was surprised when he moved by Union Turnpike and had his own apartment. I don't know how he did it.

Then there was Ira Negel, one of our friends who lived in Forest Hills. Ira was a bass player and the owner of a brown "perfecto" motorcycle jacket. He was a big guy, kind of a goon-with-a-big-heart type. He had a puffy face and was a big complainer. In the end he couldn't join the band—his mother wouldn't let him. But Ira's mother was actually cool, so it was ok. She didn't mind if all the kids hung out at her apartment, smoking pot instead of going to school.

Then, there was the mysterious Tommy Ramone. He called himself Scotty then. Scotty was a made-up name like Dee Dee. Tommy was quite a fantasy maker. Maybe coming to the US from Hungary made him appreciate the simple things—he certainly had more gratitude than most people. I was more self-destructive. I couldn't see the sense in trying

Joey and Dee Dee Ramone /*CORBIS*

LOBOTOMY

to make anything work if I could break it. For a while I used to live with Tommy in Debbie Harry's apartment. I had to admire how Tommy would place importance on the need for decent, human, rational survival, unlike anyone else in our group of friends. Tommy would go to the store and buy himself some hamburger meat and potatoes and cook them, trying to make himself a meal, and I would be laying on a mattress with half a pint of blackberry brandy, watching him cook. I just couldn't relate to that at all—forget it. But it's a good quality for a roommate to be like that, rather than to be like I was.

By the time Tommy was seventeen, he had been through one series of bad luck after another. The story goes that a gang of kids in Forest Hills put Tommy (Scotty) through some sort of humiliating experience and he became very nervous after that. Once he insisted that we get up and leave a House of Pancakes on Long Island without finishing our meal. No one knew why.

He had a girlfriend called Claudia and they were both heavy smokers. Nobody wanted them smoking in the van. Later, Tommy couldn't stand it in the van for ten hours, not having a cigarette, and everybody giving him an attitude about it. One day he just said, "Forget this guys, goodbye. I'll go smoke where I wanna smoke."

Forest Hills was starting to make me nervous as well. It got so that I had to take a couple of reds and drink a pint of Gallo wine before I took the walk down 108th Street to Richie's parents' apartment in Lefrak City. I was completely happy when I sniffed a tube of glue or a bottle of Carbona—

it took you out as far as you could go. When I was high I would call special phone numbers to listen to the *beep beep beep*. Things would go *buzz buzz buzz buzz*. Sometimes, someone would come back from the supermarket with stolen cans of whipped cream. We used to huff the gas from the whipped cream cans to heighten the effect of the Carbona and the glue.

FINALLY THE Stooges came to New York. There was an ad in *The Village Voice* that they were coming. They had a gig at the Electric Circus, which is where they have the Narcotics Anonymous meetings on St. Mark's Place nowadays. I went to that Stooges show with my girlfriend Linda and my friend Egg and his girlfriend Bennie.

Iggy didn't seem to like New York. He told everybody off. He had come on real late because he was shooting up heroin backstage and couldn't find a vein to get a hit. Iggy was famous for his dog collar, silver elbow-length gloves, and red underpants, but when he finally came out on stage he was only wearing his underpants. He threw a can of silver paint over himself and then rolled around in a bunch of glitter. Then he threw up on the floor and lay there in the vomit, rubbing it on himself.

Scott Asheton, the Stooges' drummer, had a big Nazi sign painted on the back of his motorcycle jacket. They were loud and angry. It was a great idea. They played the same song for twenty minutes that night. Once in a while they would stop. Then Iggy would shout "Take it!" and they'd do it again. It had only two chords in it and the only words to the song were

LOBOTOMY

"I want your name, I want your number." Then someone shouted "It's the ghost of Mick Jagger!" Iggy seemed upset by that remark and he walked off. The Stooges didn't come back to New York for a long time.

MY FIRST car was a Volkswagen bug. I was still living in Forest Hills and saved up the money for it by working in the mail room. Richie Stern, Johnny Ramone, and I all had jobs. We were trying hard to save money. That was our little revenge on society.

No point in writing Dad to ask for help. So I went to the newsstand on 66th Road by the Trylon Movie Theater and bought a copy of the *Buy Lines*. I thumbed through the foreign cars of the Automotive Section. Egg had warned me to get a Dodge Dart or Chevy Nova, but I wasn't listening. I was going to do it my way, but I didn't know anything about cars. I had a license, but I didn't know how to drive yet. I didn't know how to fill a car up with gas, change a flat tire, or open up the trunk or hood. Nothing.

The female police officer on my driving test felt so sorry for me that she didn't even make me take the test. She passed me and sent me on my way with a "Have a nice day, kid!" I ran into her again years later. We were both pretty tipsy. We were in a bar. We got to talking and she confessed that she only passed me because she was hoping that I would get killed in a car accident and get to end my miserable life a little bit sooner.

"Boy, it's too bad you're still around!" she added.

"I know, life has been tough on us both," I replied, stum-

64

Surviving the Ramones

bling out of McCann's Bar & Grill to the Lexington Avenue
F train that goes back to Queens. It would have been nice to
take a taxi instead of the subway once in a while, let alone
own a car. What a grim existence.

I know now that I should have listened to my friend Egg
and bought a Chevy Nova or Dodge Dart, but I bought a
Volkswagen. It was already fucked up when I bought it from
a guy in Elmhurst. When I got it back to Forest Hills I knew
that it was a lemon when the bastard thing wouldn't start up
again. I got right on the phone and called up Tommy,
because he was an expert on everything. A little while later,
Tommy pulled up in front of my Volkswagen in his Dodge
Dart. Then he ended up recharging my battery. After he left,
I drove over to the carwash on Woodhaven Boulevard. I
pulled up to the entrance and gave the dude there the
money.

I didn't know what to do; the attendant couldn't speak
English, so he couldn't tell me. So I drove the car right into
the tunnel. It was completely dark in there, so I whacked
right into the spinning brushes, which knocked the car off
the track and broke the windshield. All the soap suds spilled
into my car. It was pretty extreme. I had just smoked some
Mowwie Wowie marijuana and I was buzzed. The
Volkswagen was rolling down the tunnel, spinning off the
tracks, and I ended up being knocked unconscious. I don't
know how, but somehow I got them to replace the smashed
windscreen with an old Volkswagen front window, and vac-
uum out the soapsuds. It was still slouchy in there, but they
also recharged the battery so that I was able to put-put the

LOBOTOMY

Bug home to Forest Hills, where I parked it in front of the Hermits House.

TOMMY, JOHN, and I would go sometimes with Tommy's friend Jeff Salem to clubs on Long Island and to a bar called Nobodies in the West Village on Bleecker Street. Sometimes we would go in Tommy's Chevy Nova, but since I had a car, everybody wanted to go out in my car, so one Friday night everybody met me in front of the Hermits House. I didn't know it, but Tommy was tripping. After driving a few blocks, everybody made me pull over. They had a quick conference. Tommy got out of the Volkswagen, circled around the car and got behind the wheel. It was a roller coaster ride down Queens Boulevard. Everybody was stoned and yelling. Johnny Ramone had the Stooges' *Live at the Electric Circus* on full blast on the tape deck. Finally we were getting on the 59th Street Bridge and Tommy was getting red in the face. He was exasperated.

"Hey, guys, can you lower the music?" Tommy said. "I am tripping on LSD. Those Stooges songs are freaking me out. You don't want to run me off the road."

That was like the signal for things to get worse.

"What's the matter, Tommy? You don't like the Stooges?"

Ho, ho, ho. I lit up a joint of Chiba Chiba Colombian Gold. I was having a good time until I noticed a burning rubber smell. It was the car, not the marijuana. The car was on fire. The electric system had gone, and smoke was pouring out of the engine, which, in a Volkswagen, is in the back. Everybody started shouting with glee. In two more minutes, the car stopped running completely. Since the rest of the 59th Street Bridge is on a downward angle, we were able to coast into Manhattan anyway. We left the car on the sidewalk, where it smashed into one of Bloomingdales' windows on 59th and Third, crushing the dummies in the store window to death. We continued our journey when we caught the F train at 53rd and Lexington to 8th Street and Sixth Avenue.

EVENTUALLY I moved to Manhattan because it's such a hassle to go back and forth from Queens to the city. I got a small walk-up apartment on 85th Street and Second Avenue, and I got a new pet dachshund that I named Glenda.

When I started taking drugs, my manic nervous energy turned from nervous twitches, tapping on tables with pencils and making coo coo bird noises, into inspirations for songs. I was prepared to take LSD, speed, and grass if necessary. My mind was like a time bomb anyway. Ready to explode, with demons lurking about the edges of it to protect me from reality. I was composing all through my pre-teen and early teen years in this way. I had the heavy wahwah, screeching feedbacks, vocal melodies, and all the drum parts to hundreds of songs written out in my mind. It was all mental. I filed them all away in my head, locking the parts together to form the first songs I ever came up with. These were power rock songs. My musical abilities were too limited at the time for me to compose any other way. It was all in my imagination.

None of these songs will ever be documented, but it was a good way for me to dream myself out of the daily grind.

LOBOTOMY

One of the songs I wrote at this time, maybe my first, was called "I Can't Do It":

> *I can't do it*
> *I can't do it*
> *I can't do it*
>
> *I can't change tomorrow*
> *At the stairs to hell*
> *I can't change tomorrow*
>
> *I can't do it*
> *I can't do it*
> *I can't do it*
>
> *I can't hold on to my hand.*

Another song went like this:

> *Home is where hell is*
> *Home is where hell is*
> *Home is where hell is*
>
> *And now I am home*
> *I am with my friends*
> *Having a good time*
> *Have a tube of glue*
> *Take a tab of sunshine*

Surviving the Ramones

Home is where hell is
Home is where hell is
Everything's so bright
Everything's this way
Everything's this way
It's going to be alright
It's going to be alright
Tonight
Tonight
Tonight!

A bad breakdown inspired me to write "Questioningly" which I composed on a folk guitar, and then insisted on playing it for my mother after I had it worked out.

"Mom, Mom," I shouted into the living room from the hallway of her apartment in Forest Hills. "Can I play something for you?"

She listened to me play it as we sat in front of the TV set. I could tell that she was very surprised that I could write a song.

"How did you do that?," she asked me.

"I don't know," I said.

Then I wrote my first punk rock song on my solid body electric guitar. It was an old K solid body guitar which I bought at one of those pawn shops on 8th or 9th Avenue. I took that guitar with me wherever I went—from Brooklyn to uptown Manhattan, from Forest Hills to Queens. The song was called "I Don't Wanna Get Involved With You." In the next year or so I experimented with a few different musical projects and I also started writing more songs. I soon came up with "53rd & 3rd," "Loudmouth," "I Don't Wanna Go Down to the Basement," "Now I Wanna Sniff Some Glue," and "I Don't Wanna Walk Around With You." They just kept coming out.

Who knows where my inspiration came from? I was observing my everyday life situations and writing about them without trying to over-glorify them.

Sometimes I would go back to Forest Hills to see Johnny Ramone and Joey. I tried to start my own band in the city, called Satyricon, but it was a complete disaster. These kids thought I could be a leader. It was one thing having fun in my apartment on little amps, but once we got in a rehearsal studio everything just fell apart.

Then I answered an ad in Andy Warhol's *Interview* magazine for a guitar player for the Neon Boys, a band featuring Tom Verlaine and Richard Hell, but it wasn't what I wanted. Later, when Richard Lloyd joined them in Television, they were really good.

WHEN THE New York Dolls were playing in Manhattan, it was Beatlemania all over again. Every creep in town started a rock'n'roll band. I was really happy seeing the New York Dolls playing. They inspired some kind of rock'n'roll feeling in me. We thought Johnny Ramone was a good guitar player. No one else did at that time. Tommy was very particular about that kind of stuff and had a real dislike for Johnny Thunders because of his guitar playing. But I liked Johnny

Thunders for his guitar playing and his songwriting. But the thing that impressed me most was his harmonies. Like on "Chatterbox," that Minnie Mouse harmony thing, I always liked that. But I don't think I really realized how great he was until the Heartbreakers started. I think because his image was so great in the Dolls, that I forgot about how good he was.

Before the New York Dolls broke up in 1973 or 1974, Malcolm McLaren had come over to New York to try to rescue them. He put them in red patent leather and booked them at the Hippodrome, a club in midtown Manhattan. In some ways it was their most professional gig, but it didn't get them anywhere—booze, broads, and bad luck had already killed them off.

After the Dolls split up, the little rock'n'roll scene in Manhattan died out a bit and it was hard to find anywhere to play. Lenny Kaye, Buzzy Linehart, and Patti Smith played Max's Kansas City, but that was about it. Then Television started up and it paved the way for Blondie, and the Ramones.

Take It!

Johnny Ramone and I really had no intention of

ever playing in groups again. We both had bitter experi-

ences of other groups we had been in before the Ramones

started. We were happy just taking the subway to work

every day, going to Chock Full o' Nuts and to the Metropole

for lunch to watch the go-go dancers and drink a beer.

LOBOTOMY

Joey had a band called Sniper. He was trying to break into the New York "glam" circuit that was happening around then—groups like The Harlots of 42nd Street, The Fast, Teenage Lust, and Kiss. Tommy (Scotty), Jeff Salem, and Monte Melnick also had a group called Butch with the drummer from Dorian Zero.

The glitter look took a lot of upkeep and the gear was expensive. We would get custom-made snakeskin boots sent from England via Granny Takes a Trip in New York. Johnny Thunders and Tommy Ramone both went to London to get the right stuff to be the top flashmen about town. Johnny Ramone had an exact replica of the James Williamson outfit with the leopard collar that James wore in the Stooges' *Raw Power* stage. John also had silver lamé pants from Granny Takes a Trip that he wore for the first few Ramones gigs.

Joey and I would sometimes hang out in this unmentionable dive on Queens Boulevard called Gildas. Every time we went there I would get very drunk. I don't know how Joey got me home. Home was crashing on the floor of his mother's art gallery on Queens Boulevard near the Trylon Movie Theater. Joey's band Sniper used to rehearse there in the basement of the store. Once Joey bought some fruit and vegetables at the grocery store and used them to do a painting. He churned them in a blender and painted with them—you could either look at the painting or eat it. He was quite the artistic type. He also liked to tape thunderstorms on a reel to reel tape recorder.

I went to see a Sniper concert once when they performed with Suicide somewhere in Manhattan. It was a weird night.

They did a cover of the Rolling Stones's "Let's Spend the Night Together." Joey was called Jeff Starship then. Forgive me if I don't have it exactly right. Could it have been Jeffry Starman? Well, it was a long time ago. Anyway, he was wearing pink patent leather trousers, a silver lamé top, a pink feather boa, custom platform boots from Granny Takes a Trip, and he was singing into the mic like he had been doing it all his life. It was quite impressive.

When I first saw Alan Vega and Suicide, I pulled out my 007 knife and palmed it behind my wrist. To be frank, I was a little worried. If Iggy had created a Frankenstein, it was Alan Vega. When Alan jumped into the sparse audience, it was a bit too much for me. I didn't know what was going to happen. He's a very serious performer.

Later, Joey and I went to Max's Kansas City to check out Suicide one more time. No one was there that night but Joey, me, and a beautiful blonde in heavy S & M gear. About six or seven minutes into Suicide's set, she walked up to the right side of the stage next to some huge speakers and stood there frozen in space. The noise and the atmosphere were pretty tense. It was buzzing and flashing. Then the girl started smacking her head on the speaker cabinet, breaking the flesh. Blood was coming out of her head and she kept doing it, over and over, really hard. Eventually she stopped and just stood there with blood dripping down her face, listening to Suicide play.

Finally the Stooges came back to New York to play. They booked a show at Max's Kansas City, but had to cancel. Iggy had thrown himself down the stairs and cut himself pretty badly with a broken bottle, because he wasn't happy with how things were going.

Around this time we started to take our first baby steps as the Ramones. Like a lot of the New York groups, we took our inspiration from going to see the New York Dolls at the Oscar Wilde Room at the Mercer Arts Center and the Diplomat Hotel in Times Square. After the Dolls broke up, there were still a bunch of creeps who needed a scene.

I GUESS it's only natural that Joey, Johnny, Tommy, and I would start a band. No one else was exactly welcoming us with open arms into the Forest Hills musical community. They said we couldn't play. Years later, Johnny Ramone and I would laugh about how someone like Doug Scott, a local guitar player in Queens, could play Led Zeppelin's "Dazed and Confused" at sixteen years old and still never amount to anything. I couldn't even play the Stooges' "No Fun" and I achieved fame and fortune in the music business.

By then, even Johnny Ramone was impressed that things were happening in New York. Then one day, instead of going for lunch at the Metropole, we went over to Manny's Guitar Store on 48th Street to look at guitars. When we were walking down the street, John and I ran into Mickey Zone from The Fast. We told him we were going to take the plunge.

We ended up with a Dan Electro bass for me and a baby blue Mosrite for John. John tricked them at Manny's like he did the waitresses at Chock Full o' Nuts. We took them back to Queens, Johnny with his Mosrite stuffed in a Granny

Takes a Trip shopping bag, and they became the guitars we started the band with.

Tommy and Monte Melnick got a rehearsal for us at Performance Studios near Max's in Manhattan. We tried to figure out songs from other records, but no dice. I still don't know how we got it together. I had no idea how to tune or play a bass. Eventually Johnny would show me the bass parts to my own songs, because I had absolutely no idea how they went on the bass. All I knew was the E.

Initially the band was me on bass and vocals, John on guitar, and Joey played the drums. The first time we tried to play, we waited and waited for Joey to get ready. Finally we just started cranking it out. I was so drunk I fell over backwards and whacked my amp. It started fizzling and then stopped working. We did our first show with the Fast at Performance Studios. For the second show, no one came back.

Monte was fed up because we were so messy, but he let us come back once a week to rehearse. Eventually he became our sound man, and then tour manager—he didn't want to be called road manager. Our first manager, Danny Fields, gave Monte the job of tour manager after our first big out-of-town gig at the Tomorrow Theater in Youngstown, Ohio in June 1976. We first met Stiv Bators and the Dead Boys that night. It was a bad night—we had about ten people there. Danny said if Monte got us the money—$750— he could be tour manager. We got paid.

Joey had written some songs, like "I Don't Care," "What's Your Game," and "Here Today, Gone Tomorrow." He ended up becoming the lead singer because he knew the words. We then asked Harry, the drummer from Dorian Zero, to join the band, but he wouldn't play with us. That was a rank on the Ramones, but we shrugged it off. Tommy started playing the drums because no one else would do it for us. It was a last-ditch attempt to salvage a so-far unsuccessful musical career. Tommy completed the original line-up. After one of our early rehearsals, Tommy and I went into the studio office and had a talk. "What do you think we should call the band?" he asked me. "Oh, how about the Ramones?" I replied. I wasn't that serious, but the name stuck. Then everyone in the group took Ramone as a surname and we became the Ramones.

THE NEXT gig we played was with Blondie, who were called Angel and the Snake then, and with the Savage Voodoo Nuns. It was first time we'd played at CBGB's and we weren't ready for it. Tommy had booked us there. It was a let-down. It didn't seem as glamorous as Max's or the Mercer Arts Center. When we loaded in for the soundcheck, we had to watch out for rat, mice, and dog shit on the floor. It was the pits. Especially Hilly Kristal, a big fat guy, who ran the place and apparently never bathed. His wife, Karen Kristal, managed CBGB's and hated the Ramones more than she hated CBGB's. It was very aggravating and very unfriendly. As soon as you walked in off the street, the smell of fermenting beer was so powerful that it made you want to walk out backward. They didn't have any toilets, so the audience just pissed where they stood.

Surviving the Ramones

The first show we did at CBGB's was ok. The place was filled with drag queens who had spilled over into CBGB's from the Bowery Lane Theater. They were great to us and helped us through the show, sort of making believe for us, and it was very cabaret-like. The audience were making cat-calls, wolf whistles, and clapping dramatically to each act. It must have been a lot of fun to have been there that night. The Ramones were a very theatrical group then—like a play set to loud, sick music. We had two Mike Matthews amps from Electro Harmonics set up on chairs. They had four tens in them and were very hot-roddish.

When we sauntered on stage, I plugged in my bass and took a look around through the grim stinky haze in CBGB's. There was an ugly full-length poster of Marlene Dietrich pasted on to one wall next to the stage. The audience looked like a bunch of glowing Jack o' Lanterns sitting on a grave-yard fence on Halloween night. We played about fifteen minutes and were immediately a success. People were just dying to hear what we did. We had a four-way chemistry that was insane.

We were trying to go from one song into another. After a mishap, someone would go "Take it!" and I'd count one, two, three, four, and we'd stumble into another number. At the end of the show, I threw my Dan Electro up into the air and let it bounce up and down a few times until it broke. I thought that was the ultimate in glamor.

Connie

I got drunk after our gig at CBGB's and as I was leaving

the club at four o'clock in the morning, I noticed this babe

sitting by the Bowery on the hood of an old car, filing her

nails. I liked her right away. She was wearing a black

evening dress, spiked high-heeled shoes and had a bottle

of blackberry brandy in her purse. She looked like an

LOBOTOMY

ancient vampire countess. Her name was Connie and her mission was to capture my soul, which she did. I spent the next few years depending on her, while the Ramones were getting famous but not making any money. We were both a lot alike—totally nuts. She was just as crazy as I was. We got kicked out of everywhere we lived because of our violent arguments.

Connie had an apartment on the first floor of a brownstone building on 16th Street. She was a little older and wiser than I was, and tried to look after me, but I was difficult. You couldn't trust me and I had to be checked up on. It was must have been exhausting having me for a boyfriend. Connie put up with a lot from me, but she was also a well-known troublemaker. She was always starting fights.

Not long after I met Connie, she started up with one of my ex-girlfriends in CBGB's. Blondie had been playing, and it had been a fun night, but Connie had to ruin it. She and the other girl ended up ranking on each other and shouting terrible names at each other. I hate spectacles, so I made a quick exit out the back door, taking one of my other girlfriends, Elaine, with me. Elaine was used to battling with Connie. They had been doing it for years over Arthur Kane, the bass player for the New York Dolls, before I'd met either of them. Once, the two of them squared off on 11th Street, when Connie caught me sneaking around with Elaine. They were both tough girls and this looked like it might become more than a verbal row.

Elaine and her mother lived on a beautiful block on 11th Street, near St. Vincent's Hospital. Once in a while they let me crash there, but I was getting on their nerves already. I could tell. I drank too much beer and raided the liquor cabinet one too many times. Elaine's mom could only take so much and finally she had had enough of me. There was trouble in the air, so Elaine took me for a walk over to Smiler's, the deli on 13th Street, to get some Colt .45 beer, which was the strongest beer you could get in the States.

Connie stepped out of nowhere as we were leaving the deli. She was swinging her handbag around her head like Bruce Lee and she had put a brick in it for effect. She wasn't kidding around. Connie and Elaine went right at it, started maneuvering for the best position and were shouting at each other. This was at the end of the glitter period in New York. It was 6:30 in the morning and we were very dressed up. I had been at the Eighty-Two Club in the East Village and had been getting into hassles all night. It was quite dramatic. Then suddenly, Connie and Elaine both turned on me, Elaine grabbing me by the collar, saying "Dee Dee, do you want me or Connie?" Then, without waiting for an answer, she punched me really hard right on the side of my head. It sent me down the sidewalk and I busted open my chin when I hit the curb. Connie thought that this was very funny, so with her bloodlust satisfied, but still slightly annoyed, she took me back home.

It wasn't long before we were thrown out of our apartment on 16th Street and home was now in something called the Village Plaza. The walls in there were painted a creepy lime green like the paint jobs in mental institutions and police stations. It smelled like green roach spray and was much more

LOBOTOMY

horrible than the Chelsea Hotel. Even most of my lowlife friends wouldn't stay there. They would stay at The Earl, where Connie and I had already worn out our welcome.

IT MAY be hard to believe but I had kept my job at the mailroom to be able to afford to go to school. My dream was to attend the Wilfred Academy of Hairstyling. I had a part-time job at Bergdorf Goodman's and I was starting to do really good. I wanted to be a colorist and start over.

Then the guy I wanted to work for, Robert Kramer at Pierre Michelle's, died. And they told me: Forget it, you can't work here anymore.

I had no family to speak of. I had fallen totally out of touch with my sister, who had gotten married when she was seventeen. Beverly was going down the drain. She could have had a great career, but my family was too rugged and everybody paid for it. She got married, stopped dancing, and that was that.

Johnny Ramone had gotten into a fight with her husband. He wanted to hang out with us. And I didn't want them to hang out. I didn't want them to be around me, or drugs, or bad people. But Beverly's husband had a condescending attitude. He was a college jock type, laughing in our faces, and calling us freaks, but then trying to imitate us and hang out. John tried to be as polite as he could. He offered to drive them home, things he would never offer anyone. Finally, he just let him have it. He pulled over and said, "That's it, I'm gonna put the boot to you."

When I went home, they got mad at me and threw me out for good.

Surviving the Ramones

I was trying to follow my working class dream and it just got interrupted. I wanted to be a hairstylist, get self-sufficient, have a roof over my head, get married, whatever.

But instead the band got popular and I fell right back into this aimless behavior with a license to do whatever I wanted. I was playing every night, and being in a band and eventually I quit working. With no job, and no family, I lived in a void of irresponsibility, nothing but more free time.

WITH ALL that free time, we were making our lives much worse than they had to be. Connie was dancing at the Metropole, the go-go place on 48th Street. She also turned the occasional trick when she could get a lot of money.

And I was her little protégé. She was about ten years older than me. I was twenty-one. She had a lot of experience. She was originally from Fort Worth, Texas. I think she had been traumatized way back. She also had lived with the GTOs, Pamela, and all those people, in California. She had been living with Jobriath at the Chelsea Hotel. He had all this money and just ended up a dope fiend; he never became the next David Bowie.

In her own way, Connie took care of me. She taught me all the tricks of the trade, but unintentionally, so I'd think it was normal: this is life and this is music. In a way she was like a soulmate or the mother I wished I would have had. She was like a friend. And she tried to be good to me, in her own way. She had a total idiot on her hands to raise.

My job was to get dope for us. It started like this: Either I was playing or I would go out all night. She was dancing.

LOBOTOMY

Whenever she came home, around five in the morning, we'd be together; we'd meet in a bar and get drunk. By noon, I would go cop for us. As soon as they were selling I'd be there. If they would have been selling earlier, I would have been there earlier.

I'd go to the B & H Dairy and try to eat something. I'd always throw up from anxiety, getting ready to cop. Sometimes you had to fight for it. The first time I went to cop we got held up and had to run for it. But this became the routine, every day, drinking all night at Max's or CBGB's, drinking horrible things like grasshoppers, blackberry brandy, and wine mixed together, then going to cop in the morning and shooting up. It was part of the thing we were all doing.

After I quit my hairdressing job I moved into the loft above Arturo's loft with Connie and Joey. I caught my first habit by the age of twenty-one. One day I thought to myself: I don't want to do dope today. I knew everybody would be doing some and I just wanted to lay off. God knows why.

Of course, I started getting sick; really sick. Jonesing bad. Dope sick for the first time. Hot-cold sweats. Weird sensations. Different states of mind. A complete physical breakdown, like pneumonia. You have only one thing that wants to live and that's the craving for dope.

Connie felt sorry for me and brought some dope over.

What chance did I have? What chance did she have with me? I wasn't supporting her. Prostitution is an addiction. I think hers had been a continuous lifestyle from day one.

- ■ ■

Surviving the Ramones

WE WOULD spend one hundred dollars a day on dope if we could. I'd go cop around Rivington, Suffolk, and Norfolk Streets—side streets around Houston in the East Village towards Delancey Street.

Sometimes Jerry Nolan, the former drummer for the New York Dolls, and I would go cop together. Jerry sometimes got dope for this weirdo called Dorian Zero, who lived uptown near where I used to live, near Third Avenue in the Eighties. He also always had a steady supply of Dioxin, a speed that you could shoot up and get with a prescription from a doctor. You put Dioxin in a little glass bottle with water and closed the lid, then you would put that in boiling water for a minute and let it cook up. Then it was ready to shoot into your vein.

Dorian could hit his parents up for money, so sometimes we would hop into a cab with him up to 48th Street to a restaurant that his father owned. That was the start of the insanity. Then, with the meter still ticking, we would head deep into New Jersey to complete the whole picture. We would end up in front of Dorian's parents' house in Cherry Hill. His parents were wealthy and connected. Their home was expensive and had seven acres of manicured lawn around it. It didn't exactly have a welcome sign outside, though, and it made me nervous. The whole deal made me nervous. Dorian would leave us outside and then go into the house to argue with his mother. We could hear him shouting terrible things at her. It would remind me of fighting with my mother, except that I never got any money from her.

LOBOTOMY

For a while dope was called Chinese Rock in New York. When you would walk around the Lower East Side, people would smirk at one another on the sidewalk and let you know with hand signals that they had the Chinese Rocks. "The Rock." It was supposed to be good luck if someone had rocks. I must have had a lot of luck.

Jerry Nolan and Johnny Thunders used to call me quite frequently. Jerry would come over to my place to pick me up and then we would go cop some dope. The Heartbreakers were just getting together with John, Jerry, and Richard Hell. I guess those guys were all dope fiends then. It was not easy to cop dope. It was unreliable, it was annoying and there were rip-offs. People would buddy up and go cop. If you went and copped for someone, you were entitled to "tap" the bag. Richard Hell had mentioned to me that he was going to write a song better than Lou Reed's "Heroin," so I took his idea and wrote "Chinese Rocks" in Deborah Harry's apartment that night.

I wrote the song about Jerry calling me up to come over and go cop. The line "My girlfriend's crying in the shower stall" was about Connie, and the shower was at Arturo Vega's loft. The intro to the song was the same kind of stuff I had put in songs like "Commando" and the chorus of "53rd & 3rd." I wrote these songs before "Chinese Rocks" and The Ramones had already performed and recorded these tunes.

By the time I got the song finished I was living on 10th Street. Jerry Nolan would come over as usual. It was perfect because the dope spot had moved to 10th Street and Avenue D, so my new apartment became a meeting place because it was so close to the action.

When Jerry was over at my place one day, we did some dope and then I played him my song, and he took it with him to a Heartbreakers' rehearsal. When Leee Childers started managing them, and got them a record deal, "Chinese Rocks" was their first single off *LAMF*. Leee was originally a photographer who took all the pictures that were on the wall of Max's Kansas City. He also managed Wayne County. The song did well too, and helped start a career for the Heartbreakers. It was dedicated to the boys on Norfolk Street, I can understand that, but the credits are false. Johnny Thunders ranked on me for fourteen years, trying to make out like he wrote the song. What a low-life maneuver by those guys! By then, I was really too fucked up to care.

Being a dope addict was the worst. It was never any fun. It gives a person every reason to be miserable so you have every excuse to do it again. Connie was only adding to my misery and I was starting to be glad when she wasn't at home and was at work, dancing at the Metropole.

A friend of mine then was Black Randy, one of the most hated punks in California. Randy would fly back and forth between Los Angeles and New York, in a Brooks Brothers three-piece suit. He was robbing these people for dope money and doing very well at it. He was a freak, a dope fiend, and a con man. The Wall Street image was a front. I would always get Randy some dope when he came by for a visit. Because he was overweight it was always hard for Randy to find a vein when he was shooting up, so it would be messy, and I would end up miserable every time he came by.

Once Randy came over to the Village Plaza with a big wad

of cash. I went to Rivington Street on my bike to cop for him. All the Puerto Rican dealers were sitting on the stoop checking me out. I was a customer, so they left me alone. I felt all right around Rivington and Norfolk Streets, but it wasn't my neighborhood and I was risking it being there. But that's where the dope was.

These cop spots were store fronts that the dealers turned into social clubs. They were painted in blood red, Day-Glo orange and green colors. There were Day-Glo devil heads painted on the walls. They would glare at you from under the black lights. Somehow these places reminded me of the Café Wha. It made it weird to cop.

The dope was sort of going along with the decorations. It was cut with Procaine. The word was that it was from Mexico. It was brown rocks. Chinese Rock. But they were saying it was South American. Clever, but silly. It was just a delusion to make it easier to get the dope into America from Thailand or wherever. It wasn't as refined as the old dope. I wish whomever was manufacturing it would have kept the dope a little smoother. We had to take what they had, or be sick, so we took it. Shooting up the dope with Procaine was like shooting up heroin while you were rushing on glue. I knew that's what I would be in for, but I copped two bundles anyway. One for Randy and one for myself. Then I rode my bike back to the Village Plaza.

Soon Randy and I were really stoned. Then Randy seemed like he was overdosing. I was very fucked up, in a heroin and Procaine daze. Randy could have died. I should have called the police, but instead I poured water over him, using the garbage can under the sink for a bucket. It worked, thank God, and soon he started coming to, but by then the whole room was flooded, which I knew would be a dead giveaway to Connie. When Randy woke up, he was pretty confused. The first thing he said was "Dee Dee, got any dope?" That's how it was.

Later, when Connie came home from dancing at the Metropole on Broadway she was pissed off.

"Dee Dee, what were you doing in here? You don't even have to tell me, you motherfucking bastard. You've been doing dope without me! This whole room is flooded. What the hell happened here?"

She didn't wait for my answer. In a flurry, she picked up a wine bottle, broke it over the radiator, and slashed me with it. It was a deep wound. There was blood all over the place. I held a towel over the cut and somehow made it to St. Vincent's to get stitched up. I took the stitches out later by myself.

A couple of weeks later, I got a blade stuck in my chest. I was trying to get away from these two guys, but they pushed me into a hallway. I was walking away as fast as I could, being as cool about it as I could, but they overtook me. "Narcotics control!" they shouted in my face. That stunned me a little, but I reacted with caution and said to them, "Show me your badges."

"What are you, a wise guy?" one of them accused me. Then they shoved me into the hallway of a vacant building. Both of them had German cat knives. One of them said "Should I stick him?" The creep he was with said, "Yeah!"

LOBOTOMY

There was nothing I could really do about it. I was just glad they didn't kill me.

A friend of mine had a loft at 6 East 2nd Street, around the corner from CBGB's, so it was very convenient for the Ramones. Mostly for Joey and me. There were three lofts in the building and a factory on the first floor. A crazy painter named Jimmy lived on the top floor. Below that was a loft that six drag queens from San Francisco called home. On the floor below that lived Arturo Vega. Arturo had had bricks thrown through his windows so many times because of bad dope deals and crazy love feuds that it's a wonder no one ever got conked in the head by one.

Behind the building was a graveyard that had been dug up by the city. Some of the corpses had been buried upright in the brick wall. Once I went down there to get a loose brick, and a dead person's hand fell out of the hole where the brick had been. The hand was all bone, but a gold and diamond ring was still stubbornly stuck on its finger. It was an old engagement ring that some sucker must have bought this broad. The diamond must have been at least two and a half carats and the money I got for it at the pawnshop kept me in dope and Hostess cupcakes for months. A lot better than the nickel bag I got twenty years later for my wedding ring on 10th Street after I left the Ramones.

So, I wasn't doing so well when the Ramones started. We were playing CBGB's over and over to survive. We kept saying we wouldn't go back but we had to.

To keep my spending on dope down, I tried to keep on the Flower and Fifth methadone program, a twenty-four-day pro-

Surviving the Ramones

gram in New York. All my creepy friends autographed the cork bulletin board for the staff. Eventually everybody was on that program. Johnny Thunders, Sid Vicious, Nancy Spungen, me . . . Most of these people are dead now. I don't want to start counting or thinking about that. I don't know how I am still alive after all the drugs I used. I am glad they had that program then. For whatever it was worth, it made my miserable life a little bit better being on it. But this kind of lifestyle sucks.

Nancy Spungen was a go-go dancer and a groupie for the Heartbreakers. Everybody slept with Nancy once, and then dumped her. Then no one wanted her around at all. She could really get to you. Once, Connie tried to set me up with Sable Star, Johnny Thunders' girlfriend, while she was in Boston go-go dancing. But I went off with some other go-go dancer that I met at a Neon Leon show at Max's. Sable wasn't that hot.

I don't remember how well I really knew Nancy. Everything happened so fast. Connie knew Nancy first, because Connie was an ex-Dolls groupie and had been around more than everyone else. Everyone had a mutual fondness for drugs, sin, and violence. The sicker the better. Like one day we went to go cop some dope like we always did, but we got ripped off. We lost our dope and our money. We were all dressed up and made ourselves look too conspicuous. I was in full Bay City Rollers gear, and Connie was in hot pants, platform boots, and a halter top. We almost started a riot on 10th Street. I was glad I had dumped my platforms a couple of months before in favor of Keds sneakers. The monster boots like Slade, the Dolls, and the Wombles wore, were impossible to run in. Connie was such a pro that she had no problem with wearing platforms—which for her could also double as weapons.

We ended up by the Gem Spa on St. Mark's Place, huffing and puffing, out of breath. As we were regaining our composure, Nancy Spungen walked up to Connie and me. She seemed very miserable and started trying to bullshit us and get our sympathy. What a laugh!

Everybody was screaming, and soon we started to walk towards Chelsea. Nancy had an apartment on 23rd and Ninth Avenue. It was on the first floor. It might have been borrowed from a trick, I don't know for sure. Soon we were all stoned. Then Nancy gave Connie money, and Connie hopped a cab to 1st Street and Avenue C. I stayed with Nancy to case her apartment or whatever, and to get a free lunch out of it. When Connie came back from copping, we all got stoned again, and then we ended up in bed and tried to do some bad things. I don't think it ended up too special, though—it's all a blur.

Connie also stole Nancy's silver dollar collection. Connie was a clever dope fiend, always scheming to make more on the sneak. Nancy was younger and just learning then. She had a big crush on Jerry Nolan, but Jerry totally ignored her. He let Nancy buy him a few bags of dope, but that's about it. She was too much of a hassle. Also you could get a bad reputation hanging out with Nancy. On the bathroom wall in CBGB's there was some bad shit written about her by the other girls, who all hated Nancy.

Surviving the Ramones

Sometime around then I escaped from Connie with a girl that lived in the loft above Arturo Vega's loft. We both wanted to get away from 2nd Street and found an apartment in the *Village Voice* rental ads. I picked it out. It was on 10th Street, right in the dope area. Even though we were going out together and living together, I still didn't know much about her. She started going to some "job" every day. It was strange, but fine with me. When she was at work, Jerry Nolan started to come over to do dope and then he started bringing Johnny Thunders over.

One day my girlfriend stayed home. No matter—she was a big Johnny Thunders fan and was thrilled when John and Jerry came over. Thing is, though, she OD'd on us. We had to strip her and toss her in a bathtub filled with iced water. Soon, we sort of just forgot about her. Later, when she came to, I was the only one there.

"What happened?" she muttered in a daze.

"Oh, I threw you in the bathtub," I answered her back.

"You didn't do this in front of Johnny Thunders, did you?"

"Yes, I did!" I shouted.

Later we were in bed and she rolled over and tried to hug me. I automatically jumped right off the mattress and that did it. She went crazy and started yelling "Fuck you, Dee Dee! Fuck you! Fuck you, Dee Dee! You never let me kiss you! All you're interested in is dope!" She was right. We broke up soon after that and I went back to the loft on Second Street. Arturo took me in. I was really glad to be back at the loft. All the commotion on 10th Street was too much already.

Arturo Vega was like the Ramones' evil mom. A mean

LOBOTOMY

Latin queen that tried to pass himself off as French. Although he was really Johnny's friend, initially he let Joey and me crash in his loft and it was sort of like home for a while. Joey had a notebook where he would jot down all these ideas for songs like "Christmas in the Crypt." He also wrote "Succubus." At rehearsal me and John looked at each other with a "what kind of language is that?" look. I only found out twenty years later that it meant some kind of monster woman.

Surviving the Ramones

Joey wrote the way I wrote. I don't think he knew anything really about guitar chords, or the verse, chorus and intro. Somehow he just banged out these songs on two strings of a Yamaha acoustic guitar and then Johnny Ramone would struggle his best to interpret it. Johnny would show me the bass parts to my own songs because I had no idea how they went on the bass. But it came out very strong when we all did it, so I guess we knew we all had shortcomings and that's why John and Tommy couldn't give me and Joey all the songwriting credit. But Tommy Ramone wrote "I Wanna Be Your Boyfriend" and we could have made a million dollars on it, because the Bay City Rollers wanted to do it. But that's another story. I remember with "Listen to My Heart," after I showed it to everybody and we agreed to do it, Tommy said, "Oh, it doesn't have a middle eight in it." So I just wrote the middle eight on the spot. Tommy couldn't believe I could do that.

Anyway, I would be at Arturo's loft if I was nowhere else. I knew Connie would go there to look for me with a peace offering of dope. I slept there on a mattress that Arturo put for me in a corner behind the Ramones banner which he had hung up to divide the loft and give himself some privacy from Connie, Joey, and me. Arturo ended up with Joey and me twenty-four hours a day. He put up with a lot of craziness but he was crazy too. Eventually I think he formed a resentment towards me—which lasts to this day. We will never shake hands or be friends or anything. But back then he was trying to put up with it for the sake of art. Yes, art. He was some kind of a mad, but very talented, artist. And very cool too. He saw punk as some sort of a brand new canvas to splash paint

LOBOTOMY

on. He became the Ramones lighting director, T-shirt design-er, and graphic artist and toured with the band for a long time.

My friend Egg had been over when I was out, and was leaving New York to move to Cleveland. He had come over to say good-bye, but I wasn't there, so he left a candle that he had made himself by the bed. What a treat, I thought, when I saw it. Egg left me a present. Wow! I was in such a good mood. I also remembered that I had a very, very power-ful Thorazine pill that my counselor at the Flower and Fifth methadone program had given me for an extra special treat. Connie had warned me not to take it, and was watching me, so I had hidden it until she went away. I am set tonight, I thought. I have my candle and my pill. This is great. I lit the candle and took the pill and polished it off with a modest pint of Gallo port.

I felt happier than I had been in some time, but my hap-piness didn't last. I don't know what was up with that candle, kind of like putting a hat on the bed. I don't know, a curse, a mojo, whatever. But it was negative, not cool, and it sucked. I realized my other girlfriend, Elaine, was in there with me. I was too weirded out to be romantic or kiss and was just quite content to lay there in a daze. Shortly, though, Elaine informed me that Connie had joined us. She was in there as well, and feeling lovable. *I don't trust her*, I thought. The Thorazine had knocked me for a loop, and I was helpless. It was extreme and there was nothing I could do. It was like being in a straitjacket, so I just grinned that grin that I do when all is not well.

Soon it got worse. Elaine and Connie were pissed off at me and not paying attention to the candle which had melted and set light to the floor. Before we knew it, the fire started spreading throughout the loft. Connie was beside herself with glee and jumped up and started throwing cans of paint around to fuel the flames. She threw a can of paint at me, then splashed one of Arturo's paintings.

"Everyone gets a paint job!" she was shouting. "We're all gonna die!" She was thrilled. Then I thought I saw Elaine sneaking up behind Connie and trying to push her into the corner of the loft that was really ablaze and where the floor was caving in. But Connie was too quick for her. It was horrible. "Why me?" I was thinking to myself. That creep, Egg, who had given me the candle, had moved to Cleveland.

Sometimes it seemed never ending and I was stuck there to deal with one problem after the next. Like Jimmy, the demented drag queen downstairs. What a bastard. It's a wonder the building didn't burn down a million times because of the lowlifes he was bringing up to his loft on the top floor. Bricks would sometimes sail through his window, too, like the ones through Arturo's. It was weird, but it was bold, exciting, great.

Besides being a queen, Jimmy was also an artist. He was even crazier than Arturo Vega. He was a big boozer and a real sick guy or a girl—to him, it was the same. One day his wife came home and found him in drag. The bastard was lying on the couch dead drunk and stoned. He had a wedding dress on and eye make-up, blusher, and red lipstick and a blond beehive bouffant wig. He was quite nasty. The shouting

LOBOTOMY

started right away. You could hear it from Arturo's loft and from down on the street, where a crowd was gathering to listen.

"Queer motherfucker!"

"Fuck you, Mary!"

"You wish!"

"Get lost, sister."

Finally she left and we never saw her again. Everybody on the street let out a big cheer. Jimmy then came to the window and promised a big party for all, to celebrate his good fortune.

After his wife left, Jimmy made good on his promise and threw a party like he said he would. He invited all the bums on the Bowery. It turned into a heavy drug and booze scene. Then he took some Thorazine and completely lost his mind. He turned control of the household over to a brute called Margo, a very highly feared and tough drag queen who specialized in ripping off sailors on the Bowery and holding up drug addicts in the neighborhood. It all went downhill on 2nd Street from that time on. Having Margo for a neighbor was a curse. She was really horrible, so noisy and creepy that I started to feel like life wasn't worth living. The little building I called home was turning into the pits. I was getting paranoid. There goes my security, I thought. This can't last much longer. They're gonna come and throw us on the street any minute. Arturo was a wreck.

Connie said that if she had to fight Margo, it would be like a cat on a dog, whatever that meant. It was frightening and things in our building were definitely getting worse. There

100

was a killing. A couple of them—stabbings. They were killing cats up there, I know that for sure, because they would throw their half-eaten carcasses out the window. It was disgusting.

Then Jimmy ran out of money. He got stuck up there with no more booze, no heat in the building because the city turned off the gas and electricity because he hadn't paid the bills. All his creepy friends started to get angry. Jimmy's guests were all real down-and-out alcoholics and perverts. No one gave a shit. They were all chopping up the furniture for firewood and building campfires on the floor for heat and to cook rats they caught when no one had a cat. It was nuts.

Finally Jimmy convinced everybody that he had hidden a lot of cash behind one of the bricks in the wall. So everybody started aimlessly chopping holes in all the walls. They stubbornly started searching in the basement for the money. After a while, Margo went down there to see what was going on. I didn't go down there to investigate what happened. All I know is that I never saw the rest of them again. I didn't ask Jimmy about it because he was too busy getting drunk and I didn't ask Margo because I always tried to avoid her even though she liked me. Leave well enough alone, I thought.

Finally, Connie gave me the ultimatum. She had come at me with a butcher's knife the day before. Somehow I had reached out my arm automatically and grabbed a broom handle in my hand, and I managed to sweep the blade from Connie's left hand. I don't know how.

"Now listen here, sweetie, Connie. Please darling, please calm down. Please, keep the knives in the kitchen. No more stunts today, ok? I am drained. I can't take any more. I am really tired."

Connie looked at me with glowing-yellow hateful eyes. A look that could stop a cop.

"Dee Dee, you queer motherfucker," she shouted at me.

"Connie, what's up?" I shouted back at her.

"Well, Dee Dee, you stupid creep, what do you think? It's that fag Margo upstairs. I can't stand it. Fuck everything! I need some dope now to cope. I hate it! Do something, now!"

I knew I had to face Connie or face Margo. What a choice. At times like this, I just lose all feelings in me. I marched out into the stairwell. I had on a heavy pair of jack-boots and kicked a post from the railing to use as a club. Then I walked into Jimmy's loft—without knocking or any-thing—and sorted Margo and those freaks out. But that experience left me played out, and when Connie threw a beer bottle at Mark Mendosa, the Dictators' bass player, at CBGB's, the next day I went back to Queens to rest and hide out for a week.

LIFE STARTED getting even more insane every day. The atmosphere was dangerous and intoxicating. It's a good thing for me that the Ramones started touring. We were doing shows in little towns in the Northeast most nights. That gave me a chance to avoid the East Village for a while. It got too hard for me to keep up a dope habit, so I switched to booze. Then all I had to deal with were my hangovers—instead of making it back and forth from Norfolk Street without getting stabbed, ripped off, or arrested. Basically, I was turning into a junkie. I think the Ramones really saved me, got me off the street.

Every musician I knew from that time said the same thing—"Oh, I was so happy when we started touring, I had somewhere to live—in the hotel every day." But then when it stopped, there was nowhere to go. Nothing to eat. The Ramones were like my family and my security. I could go and get a meal and a place to live and a place to play, and it was good.

Even early on, my relationship with the rest of the Ramones was always strained because I think they couldn't understand me. I probably threatened the security of the band because of my wandering traits. I wouldn't conform to anything. Everything immediately outlived its value to me. I don't know how it could have been any different. There was no one to show me any other way.

I never had a childhood. I couldn't have a band. I had to get somewhere to live. I was trying to set an unattainable standard for myself and I think that what set me apart from John, Joey, and Tommy was that they seemed to have something I didn't. I don't know what their real family life situations were like, but I felt like an outsider, because at the end of the day, I really didn't have anywhere to go, and they did. Tommy wouldn't even let anybody in his apartment. He didn't want anybody in there. He would answer the door and peer at you from behind the door. You had to wait outside. John's parents were always really friendly to me. I really got along with them. His mother and father really liked me. But I always thought the other guys had a security that I didn't have.

I had no place to go and grow up. I think that's why I had to have a secret life of my own, in the middle of all this madness.

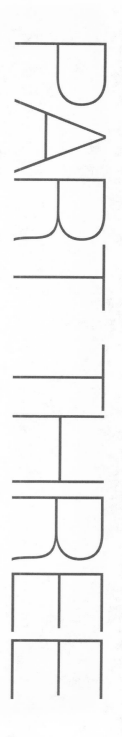

**Ramones
Leave Home**

Dee Dee, 1977

Rock and Roll Star

It all happened so fast. The Ramones made a name for

themselves in New York City, playing regularly at CBGB's,

Max's Kansas City, and other underground venues. People

were making a serious fuss about us.

Seymour Stein signed us to Sire Records for the sum of

$6,000. Typically, I didn't know what the hell I was doing.

LOBOTOMY

I just went into Arturo's loft and signed a contract; I didn't even know what I was signing. I gave John and Tommy all this publishing from my songs. Tommy had his brother represent us as a lawyer. Seymour Stein and Danny Fields signed us; and they're as cheap as they come. Real cheapskate stuff.

Still, Seymour was a very smart man. He invented the theory behind selling alternative music and starting alternative labels in the US. He started by buying back publishing rights and putting out bands like Fleetwood Mac and the Climax Blues Band, and using the money from that to put into bands like the Talking Heads, and later Soft Cell and Madonna.

And at the center of it all were the Ramones. We really did carry the tradition of rock and roll, we kept it alive.

Now it makes me feel good, *now* I understand how much we influenced people, but at the time I didn't have any real self-esteem. I just thought of myself as totally insignificant.

The first album only took a couple of days to record in February 1976 at Plaza Sound in Radio City Music Hall. It was released in April.

The reviews were good, but sales of the first LP were not exactly spectacular, and because of our reputation, many promoters were still reluctant to book us. It almost felt like it never came out, because it was so anticlimactic to all the fuss about the band.

Then when it did start to catch on, I got scared. The bigger and more powerful it became, the more afraid of it I became. "It isn't mine," I thought. It meant I had to give up my freedom and be a part of something and commit.

Surviving the Ramones

And I didn't know how to do that. I'm used to being a loner. I lived in a total fear of having to explain myself and my situation.

I couldn't handle the attention. Instead of being appreciative and working on playing and improving myself I just thought "Oh, I'm cool," and I hit the street as a drug addict. I didn't know any other way.

It's Alive!

For the next three years, the Ramones toured almost

non-stop. I liked touring. I would try to look for excitement

and some fun wherever we went. I kept myself clean. I felt

a sense of security. I got my per diem every day, I had a roof

over my head, and no worries. And my hotel room was my

little home. I enjoyed being independent and, unlike the rest of the band, I knew how to get around in Europe. They hated it there.

But I was never homesick. I never wanted to come back to the States.

WE WERE making a bigger impact in England, where the album quickly reached number one on the import chart, thanks to regular airplay on John Peel's evening show on Radio 1. One British critic even hailed us as the saviours of rock'n'roll.

I guess the climate in the UK was much more inclined toward a band like the Ramones. The UK punk movement, centered around the Sex Pistols, was about to take off. Punks were running up and down Kings Road, fighting Teds. And Malcolm McLaren had his clothing shop, Sex, right there.

We flew to England in July of 1976, the weekend of the Bicentennial, to play two shows with the Flamin' Groovies. The first was at Dingwalls and then on Independence Day, July 4, 1976, we played to 2,000 enthusiastic fans at London's Roundhouse, our largest audience so far. I remember it was a very hot summer in England that year.

Danny Fields, our first co-manager, showed us around town. Danny was a photographer and a member of the Warhol set, and he had also managed the Stooges and Jonathan Richman. He was friendly with Linda Stein, wife of Seymour Stein, owner of Sire Records, who also co-managed the band.

Our first look at London consisted of walking around Hyde Park at four in the morning. It was very low budget stuff. That's how Danny showed us around town.

Then we were on our own. I went off to Camden Market where I bought all the Doctor Feelgood and Eddie and the Hot Rods singles. I also bought "Keys to Your Heart" by the 101'ers. It was very exciting for me to buy these records. They were on weird labels that no one had heard of, and had cool picture sleeves. It was still so in touch with proper rock-'n'roll. The Rock On stall had a Teddy Boy feel to it. It was like being in a time warp seeing this fifties rock'n'roll scene and then to be opening up for the Flamin' Groovies, who dressed head to toe like the Beatles.

It was at the first show at Dingwalls, a small club in the middle of Camden Market, that I got my first introduction to English punks. At the soundcheck I met Mick Jones and Paul Simenon from The Clash. Paul had paint flecks on his shoes. It was artistic, in a graffiti-style way. They all had short hair, but didn't seem mod. Johnny Rotten and Sid Vicious were also there that night. It wasn't my favorite show that we played in England or anything like that, but it was a great start. Meeting the Sex Pistols individually, before they had a band, you would never have thought of them as musicians. But the Clash was obviously going to be a serious band.

The next night we played the Roundhouse with The Stranglers and the Flamin' Groovies. As we were driving up to the Roundhouse for our soundcheck, someone said, "There's Sid Vicious!" Through the permanent drunken haze I was in, I could see Sid standing by himself on the sidewalk, looking a bit off in space. It cheered me up to see him, some-how. He was a show all in himself, standing there outside the Roundhouse, wearing baggy red-loon pants, a black fishnet top, eye make-up, black nail varnish, and short blue-black hair that wasn't spiked up yet. I met him later on that night and we hit it off immediately. Sid liked the Ramones and started following me around. Later when he joined the Sex Pistols, he started wearing ripped jeans like Joey Ramone and a Ramones–style leather jacket.

The Ramones kept playing England so much around then that it's hard to keep it all straight. But I think the next time we were in England was in 1977. On a day off I can remember going to Brighton to see The Clash. It was one of the first times I had heard reggae music. I remember this strange sight of a thousand punks on the dancefloor, dancing between band sets to this reggae music blaring from the disco. I'd never seen anything like it before.

I was having a good time until I ran into Nancy Spungen on the balcony of the theater. She started shouting enthusiastically in my ear about Sid this and Sid that. She said that Sid was the star of the Pistols. That Sid was her new boyfriend. I couldn't hear the Clash at all because Nancy was shouting in my ear about Sid. It was too much. I became exhausted by all the commotion. I started entertaining the thought of pushing her off the balcony. Nancy ended up buying me off with a bottle of brandy. I hate to cliché her, but she was a pest, a party crasher.

The next night there was a party at the Country Cousin on the King's Road. The place was hot and there was no air-conditioning. No matter how much cheap warm wine and beer they dispensed to the party-goers it couldn't seem to quench their thirst. Everyone was drinking themselves silly. It was pretty decadent. I noticed Captain Sensible, the bass player from the Damned, as soon as I walked in. He was sitting at a fancy, expensive piano, and threatening to play it for us. He was dressed in a ballerina tutu and old Doc Marten's that someone had spray-painted white. Everyone was there, from Gaye Advert to Marc Bolan. I couldn't find any dope, though, until finally some German gentleman that I met at the party laid twenty grams of speed on me. I didn't know what to do with it at first. Then, with Sid trailing along behind me, we headed to the toilet to figure it out.

There was vomit everywhere. On the floor, in the sink, and overflowing from the toilet bowls. *This is sick*, I thought to myself. Sid and I both immediately threw up as well. I hadn't seen anything yet, though, not until Sid produced a horrible syringe with old blood caked around the needle. I gave Sid some of the speed and he tapped it into the syringe to load it up for a hit. Then he stuck the needle into the toilet and drew up water from the bowl into the hypo so he could coldshake the speed that was in the outfit. The water had vomit, piss, and snot in it. Sid didn't seem to think that this was in any way out of the ordinary. His main concern seemed to be to shoot up and was prepared to put up with any amount of discomfort for the rush. *Now I've seen it all*, I thought.

While Sid was finishing his shot, John Cale walked into the bathroom. He was stinking drunk, but could tell right away what we were up to. He tried to be coy.

"Dee Dee, got anything?" he asked me in a friendly, nonchalant way.

"Oh, I don't know," I replied, lying through my teeth. "Ask Sid. Sid has some."

LOBOTOMY

The next thing I knew, Sid was shaking on the floor having a fit. Green foam was coming out of his mouth. His eyes were popping out of his head. It was terrible, so I ran back to the bar to get help. In the confusion, I slipped and fell down the exit stairwell, knocking myself unconscious. Finally, I was taken back to the hotel in an ambulance.

The next day I met Sid. The Sex Pistols were playing a gloomy venue outside of London at some college or university. Sid and I were talking on the balcony outside the dressing room, looking down over the audience in the theater.

"Sid," I said to him, as I scanned their backline on the stage below, "you guys don't have lights or a P.A. set up."

"Right, ain't it," he replied.

"Yeah, right," I answered back.

There were a few thousand people in the place. How was anyone going to see or hear them when they went on? The audience was really geared up for it and the atmosphere was partylike, but backstage it was a little depressing. Sid asked me if I wanted a beer and then went into the dressing room—from which he had been banned—to fetch one for me. He came back with the beer and it was already opened. I didn't trust this because the Ramones always put a few drops of piss in anything they gave their guests to drink after the show, as a little joke to laugh about later. I figured that the Pistols would do the same thing, so I avoided Sid's generosity. When no one was looking I poured the beer into their manager's empty glass; he drank it down in one gulp.

"I know Malcolm doesn't like me, so I am going, Sid," I said, and made my escape.

The same thing had happened the previous year when Johnny Rotten had come backstage to see us at the Roundhouse. Johnny Ramone was very friendly to him, shook his hand, patted him on the back, and asked him if he wanted a beer. Johnny Rotten took it from Johnny Ramone and then while John was smirking, he drank it down in one gulp. I was holding my breath. This is unbelievable, I thought to myself. When Johnny Rotten left, we couldn't believe that he'd come to see us.

To this day I think that the Sex Pistols' album is one of the best albums of all time. They got an enormous amount of press. And they barely played. Malcolm would always put them in impossible political situations, us-versus-them situations, live; it was one stunt after another. But the truth is they were really a good band. They weren't a bunch of monkeys. They were totally street. They couldn't protect themselves from the street. They had to walk around. And I'd come by in a limousine and see them right there on the street.

People were pitting us against them and them against us. The Sex Pistols were selling more records and getting more famous but after a disastrous tour of America, the Sex Pistols broke up.

MEANWHILE, THE Ramones felt like they weren't getting any respect. The British press treated us like clowns. At first, we went on the defensive and acted tough. Then, we stopped caring. The rot was setting in.

Even though we were doing well in Europe and England, life on the road with the Ramones was getting more and

LOBOTOMY

more difficult. I liked it in Europe, but the Ramones could-n't get used to it and started to hate going there, especially as English audiences liked to spit at us. We still kept going back to tour, but it wasn't any fun. There was a lot of tension between the band members. Johnny Ramone would yell at everybody when he came off stage. When we returned to the States, we would go back to playing places on the same level as CBGB's. You couldn't win. Sometimes it seemed like people just came to the show to hate us and to look for a fight.

There was also constant feuding on the road, not just between the band members but between their various wives and girlfriends. Yelling, fighting, and trouble. It was a circus. Everybody's sour behavior and power struggles never let up.

In the studio, the Ramones were quick to record. Then Joey would take a really long time to do his vocals. Everybody was saying, "Oh, you know, it usually takes a band three albums to make it." Like Aerosmith. But I just felt like they were making excuses. It was hard having all of our friends trying to figure out why the Ramones weren't more successful.

The first three albums were real Ramones albums. On *Rocket to Russia*, I didn't have to worry because Tommy was producing. I like Tommy's drumming. He was a Ringo Starr–type drummer, a quieter rock-and-roll drummer. He really had the garage sound. We're all big guys and Tommy is little; he balanced us out.

Those first three records are filled with fun memories for me. The record company wasn't putting the kind of pressure on us that they later would to get on the radio. And I wasn't thinking about what the possibilities were. I wouldn't have known how to calculate success even if I chose to. It was like the American dream. We just said, if it isn't available, we'll make it happen. Or we'll go to war. Or we'll secede. Or we'll go somewhere else. And so we just created the Ramones on a hope and a prayer and on our guts.

Then Tommy left the Ramones. I had been watching him deteriorate on the road. Tommy didn't hold up too well—he wasn't really made of the real stuff that rock stars are made of. And finally one day he was gone.

Dee Dee and Marky in Amsterdam, 1995 *Barbara Zampini*

LOBOTOMY

I went to a band rehearsal in New York and Marc Bell was there. John and Joey had asked him to join the band. We could never recapture that classic punk sound after Tommy left, but with Marc in the band we got a very hard player. Marc had been my drinking buddy before he joined the Ramones and I loved to party with him. We both started going down the road to ruin together. The two of us spelled trouble, but to me he was more fun than John or Joey and I was glad to have him in the band.

I first heard about the movie *Rock'n'Roll High School* from

Joey. Filmmaker Allan Arkush was going to direct a movie

about us for Roger Corman who made all those great B-

movies like *Death Race 2000* and *The Wild Angels.*

It was good that we got to do the movie but it wasn't

the most pleasant experience. In fact, it was horrible, real low-budget. I didn't like Vince Van Patten or the other extras in the movie. They weren't bad people or anything but they just came from a totally different world than the Ramones. They were a bunch of tennis players and we're not like that. There was not much of a social life between us and the actors; in fact, it was like day and night. They weren't even Ramones fans, except for Allan the director.

I was too broke to enjoy L.A. I was staying at the Tropicana but I had no money. We weren't at our most popular but our record company wanted us to have a new start.

The Tropicana was scary. It was too open. You had absolutely no protection from street life, and your past. People would come pounding on your door all night, wanting to know if you wanted any dope.

One night I got into a fight with my roadie and ended up in jail. Then I OD'd in the jail and they took me out of jail and I woke up in Cedars Sinai with a $3,000 bill.

During the entire shoot, I was very unhealthy mentally; I was too soggy-brained from alcohol and barbituates to concentrate, and most people's attitude toward me was: He isn't valid enough to help. There is a way to get help, to get off drugs and straighten out, and nobody felt I was worth helping.

Marc and I were drinking ourselves to oblivion, twenty double martinis a night. Booze and pills and cocaine. We were sick. It was as if we were trying to poison ourselves.

I wasn't some jaded maniac like John Belushi. I was just a moldable kid. Our manager Danny Fields is a total romantic with no conscience whatsoever. As far as the people around me were concerned, if I died it would only serve to make the group bigger. Not one person said, this is an emergency, you ought to get yourself together. I could've used some help instead of just criticism.

THE RAMONES couldn't accept Marc, and he realized it. We stopped getting along and drinking together because of the tension. By then, the Ramones had a no-alcohol policy that I couldn't conform to and neither would Marc. I started arguing with Johnny Ramone because I felt the band was blaming me for all our failures. I was the most fucked up and the weakest one in the band and I was starting to hate their guts. John and Joey were laughing at how Marc was behaving and taking a real glee in instigating his hostility toward me. They started telling him little white lies, like it was *my* decision that he didn't get any money for the T-shirts we sold. Stuff like that was really pissing me off.

Maybe John had the worst role in the band—as an authority figure—someone had to take it. But, maybe that's what made him so unpleasant. Or perhaps he was just doing everyone else's dirty work. In the music business it really is true, you don't get anywhere except by shouting, threatening, fighting, and this type of behavior. It always ends up being unpleasant. You have to fight for everything. Everything. Every single aspect of your daily life—to get a show done, get on the road, get everybody to take their positions, get the money, get it done, get out of there, get the equipment out. Someone has to do it. So John had to do a lot of that, and I think it took years off his life. No one gave him any sympathy for it, all the grief he had to put up with. But he milked

LOBOTOMY

it for all it was worth—I didn't see that happening. I saw that as Johnny Ramone's rules, Johnny Ramone's justifications, not mine.

One of the rules was that we had a dress code. We adopted the uniform of ripped jeans, bowl haircut, leather jackets, and sneakers. It was all part of being a Ramone. Once, when we flew home from Amsterdam after a long tour of Europe, I did the opposite of what everyone thought I would do. I stayed sober on the flight back home to the States and took a good look at what was going on. Marc was as drunk as a skunk and acting insane. John and Joey, and their girlfriends Roxy and Linda, were being horrible to me.

When we cleared customs at Kennedy, I walked over to John and cursed him out. I felt like I didn't want to be a Ramone any more. To me, it was bullshit. I didn't need them to tell me what to do all the time and then rail on me. I did a lot for them. I had put my life into the band, but nothing could satisfy them. They ended up creating an enemy right in their own ranks—me. It was pretty damn stupid. Especially for Roxy and Linda to start up with me. I was sick of it. I was sick of the Ramones, and the haircut as well. When I got home from the airport, I marched straight into the bathroom and cut my hair off into a Sid Vicious hairstyle. They won't like this, I thought, and made a Sid-like sneer into the mirror.

The first time I met Phil Spector was at the Whisky A

Go Go on Sunset Boulevard in Hollywood, California.

Phil was there to see Blondie who was playing that

night. Somehow I got lucky enough to have a day off from

touring and be in Los Angeles at the same time.

LOBOTOMY

Blondie and Deborah Harry were friends of mine and were starting to have some success with a song called "Denis," which Richard Gottehrer had produced. But Phil had the idea he could do better, and I think he was obsessed with stealing Deborah Harry away from Blondie, producing a record for her and making her a major star. Perhaps he was in love with her and secretly wanted to marry her, who knows?

Blondie was really good that night, and I was having a great time. Deborah Harry was smashing, and wearing one of the shortest mini-skirts I had ever seen her wear. All the boys were crowding the front of the stage, trying to get a look up her skirt at her white bikini briefs. It was all quite enjoyable and I was making it better for myself by buying round after round of drinks for all the patrons in the club. I was already so drunk by the time I got to the Whisky that when Blondie came on stage I had very little idea of what I was doing.

As excited as Los Angeles was to have Deborah Harry and Blondie finally playing in their city, I could sense that there was one sourpuss in the audience that did not appreciate what was going on. My psychic intuition was later to prove accurate, as I found out after the concert when I tried to go backstage and mingle with the band. I was stinking of rum and very tipsy. But it was no great challenge for me to find my way up the stairs to the Whisky A Go Go's backstage dressing room, as I had been there so many times before. But, as I was walking up the stairs, my way was blocked by a man holding the red velvet curtains at the top of the staircase together so as not to let me pass through. This man I can only describe as resembling Count Dracula himself. He was dressed in a batwing-type cloak, he had a black beard and mustache which gave him a devilish appearance, and his dark aviator shades gave him an aura of menace and mystery. Later I discovered that this man was the crown prince of darkness himself, Mr Phil Spector.

"Where do you think you are going?" he addressed me.

"I'm going to see Debbie now," I told him.

"Not on your life," he told me.

But at just the right moment, a drunken and stoned Jimmy Destri opened the dressing room door and everyone spilled out toward the entranceway past Phil, sweeping us inside. There was little he could do. Phil was furious, because a hot and sweaty Deborah Harry was sitting there in the dressing room, clad only in her bra and panties—she hadn't had time to change yet. I don't know if Phil had ever seen Debbie in this state before, but I sensed he didn't want anyone else to. So he was really pissed off and when he entered the dressing room and saw Debbie, freshening up her lipstick and being very friendly to me, he formed an instant bitter dislike for me, before he even knew me.

The name Phil Spector was mentioned to me again shortly upon my return to New York. Danny Fields informed us that Seymour Stein had decided that it would be good if the next Ramones' album were to be produced by Phil Spector. This was around the time the Ramones were involved with the *Rock'n'Roll High School* movie, 1978 or '79. I think the original idea for working with Phil was for him to produce the song "Rock'n'Roll High School" for the movie soundtrack. Maybe the record company thought that they could make a hit out of punk rock in the US by having Phil produce us.

By this time Seymour had really gone out on a limb for the Ramones. We still hadn't scored a hit, but no one was giving up on us and it made sense that perhaps a movie with music by Phil Spector and the Ramones would be a success. So Danny and Linda Stein invited me for a lunch/business conference at the Russian Tea Room on 57th Street, which is across the street from their management office and not too far from Studio 54.

My memory about dates and specific events is fuzzy. I was heavily into sedatives and prone to falling asleep at any time. It was hard to communicate with me—I had no interest in anything. I don't even remember the plane ride that brought me to Los Angeles for those fateful Ramones–Spector sessions. I may have already been in Los Angeles for a couple of months working on the *Rock'n'Roll High School* movie, which makes sense because I can imagine that Danny and Linda would have thought it best for us to do the album and movie simultaneously, to make the most productive use of our stay in Los Angeles.

I think I remember being in the Gold Star studio with the Paley Brothers, trying to record a song called "Come on, Let's Go" and I couldn't remember how to play it. I had done the simple bass part hundreds of times and each time I made a serious mistake. Maybe the Gold Star studios was just too historic a place for me. This was where Phil Spector created his Frankenstein experiments and the Beach Boys supposedly blew their minds.

Surviving the Ramones

In the studio there were many large hospital–type oxygen tanks, complete with face masks and valve regulators for use either as a hangover cure or to aid alertness. This was supposedly invented by Brian Wilson. Underneath the studio floor was a swimming pool which was used as an echo chamber—when Phil Spector started recording, studio techniques were still too primitive to achieve these effects normally, so he had to do things this way to get what he wanted.

I guess that's why there was an aura of underlying threat. Maybe my imagination was set off from hearing so much talk about handguns and personal bodyguards and karate techniques. Finally I finished "Come on, Let's Go," and amazingly despite the recording conditions and my immediate surroundings, the song came out quite cheerful.

Later, after I left Phil's laboratory at the Gold Star Studios, with Monte and the band, we went to meet Phil. Ed Stasium, the coproducer of *End of the Century*, escorted us to an out-of-the-way rehearsal studio in Hollywood somewhere. We tuned the guitar and bass and started struggling through "Rock'n'Roll High School." The stage was at the end of a big, long room with a very highly polished floor. When we were halfway through the song, Phil appeared and walked confidently to the center of the empty room, placed his briefcase in an open position, and, as there was no chair, crouched on the floor, peering at us from behind his briefcase. Needless to say, it had been a long day and I was losing my sense of humor and really feeling like I could use a good sleep. I don't know what Phil was doing behind his briefcase, but something seemed very suspicious to me about this type of behav-

LOBOTOMY

ior. When we finished playing the song, Phil walked over to us and congratulated us on how good the song sounded, but I still felt very ill-at-ease.

I guess this was all just one of Phil's tests to scrutinize us before agreeing to produce us. I guess the next step was for Phil to see if he could enjoy being around us. After all we would be in each other's company for quite a long time, as it takes Phil a long time to complete an album. Everybody looked beat, probably from partying every night, so we all made a polite excuse to go our separate ways and meet again the next day at Phil's mansion in Beverly Hills.

The drive to his house was up a steep highway. When we arrived, the place was like a heavily fortified mansion and we had to press a button and wait until we had cleared a security check and the roadblocks from the gateway to the house. His estate was a bit shabby and not very well kept. Maybe it was because he was a bachelor and lived there alone with his huge St. Bernard and two bodyguards. As far as I could see, his only other friend at the time seemed to be disc jockey Rodney Bingenheimer. We knew Rodney as he had The Ramones on his first show for KROQ in Los Angeles in 1976.

Once inside his home, Phil took us for a brief tour. I'm a big fan of Phil Spector's music and, as out of it as I was at the time, I was aware that I was in the presence of a great rock'n'roll legend, but he was really making me nervous. After the tour of his mansion, he left me, John, and Marc downstairs in the piano room, while he took Joey upstairs for a private conference. After about three hours I was getting restless, sitting there in that room with nothing to do except stare at John and Marc. Finally I got up off the couch and tried to find Phil and Joey to see what was up. Phil must have thought I was an intruder. I really don't know what provoked him, but the next thing I knew Phil appeared at the top of the staircase, shouting and waving a pistol. Then he practically field-stripped the thing in two seconds flat, put it back together in two more seconds flat. He had all the quick-draw, shoot-to-kill pistol techniques. Like Jimi Hendrix only with a pistol instead of a guitar.

I can't believe this, I thought to myself. *I'm bored to death, I've got to get the fuck out of here.*

"Phil," I challenged him, "I don't know what your fucking problem is, waving that pistol around and all that stuff, and trying to steal Joey away from the Ramones? I've had it. I'm going back to the Tropicana," which was the hotel on Santa Monica Boulevard where we were staying.

"You're not going anywhere, Dee Dee," Phil said.

He leveled his gun at my heart and then motioned for me and the rest of the band to get back in the piano room. Everybody sat down on the couch and had another beer. We were all very drunk by then—I was fed up, confused, and hungry. Phil was a merciless host. He only holstered his pistol when he felt secure that his bodyguards could take over. Then he sat down at his black concert piano and made us listen to him play and sing "Baby I Love You" until well after 4:30 in the morning. By 5:00 A.M. I felt as if I was going to completely lose my mind.

Two weeks later Johnny Ramone, Marky Ramone, Joey, me, Ed Stasium, and Phil Spector were in a studio in anoth-

LOBOTOMY

er secret location in Hollywood. We had been working for at least fourteen or fifteen hours a day for thirteen days straight and we still hadn't recorded one note of music. I can't imagine why, but I was getting impatient. Phil would sit in the control room and would listen through the headphones to Marky hit one note on the drum, hour after hour, after hour, after hour. It sort of reminded me of being back in Forest Hills, in Birchwood Towers with Joey Ramone in his mother's apartment, dribbling a basketball for hour after hour while Joey got it on tape.

During one lunch break a couple of days later, I asked Ed, "Where's John now?" and Ed replied "Oh, John left five hours ago. He flew back to New York."

"That's crazy," I said, "we haven't even begun recording the album."

"Well what can I tell you?" Ed told me, "I think he was trying to hide a lot of anxiety."

I went back by the soda machines and lounge area and saw Marc. "Marky," I said, "John left. He went back to New York. What do you think we should do?"

"Let's go home," Marky said.

I don't know how we did it, but somehow Marky and I managed to book a flight back home to New York that evening at seven o'clock. The next morning we were back at JFK airport. To this day, I still have no idea how they made the album *End of the Century*, or who actually played bass on it.

Chicken Beak Boy

When I wasn't touring with the Ramones, I went

home to my little basement apartment in Whitestone which

is a boring, middle-class neighborhood. I lived there ten

years, but it never felt like home. My landlord lived above

me and he wasn't exactly the rock'n'roll type. I was too

nervous to play my stereo, or play my bass through an

LOBOTOMY

Lynn Goldsmith / CORBIS

amp. Everybody was just into other things like planting crummy sunflowers all around their homes. Jesus Christ, I am more like a vampire type. It was not my kind of environment.

Then, one day, my landlord's son rang my bell. I totally freaked when I saw this little kid standing out there. I felt very uncomfortable—the whole apartment smelled of pot smoke. I told him to come back later. Soon, he was at the door again and sort of vaguely communicating to me in broken English that he was interested in guitars and stuff. I went and got one of my electric guitars and gave it to him.

"Take this," I said.

Surviving the Ramones

I was trying to do something that my father had never done for me. I didn't know what it was like to have a kid. I've never had any, which used to bother me, but it doesn't now. My life was so shitty that it was really better that I didn't bother having a family.

Although Whitestone is a nice middle-class family neighborhood, it's a total drug neighborhood, too. I had chosen it because it's the farthest town from the nearest subway stop and I didn't want to be able to get into Manhattan to cop dope. But the truth was that I could have cocaine delivered as easily as pizza. But I was mainly into smoking pot then. I was smoking about an ounce of it a day. It was causing me a lot of anxiety.

ONE OF the things that I liked about visiting a place like Amsterdam was all the things you can get there legally that you can't get in the United States. In Holland you can buy cannabis legally. The menu for marijuana is written on a chalkboard in coffeeshops to tell you what kinds are available for the day. My favorite was Zero Zero, an opiate hash that really got me stoned.

When we played the Paradiso in Amsterdam, the hash store in the club would open after the soundcheck. I would try to buy the largest amount of hash they would sell me, and would explain myself with hand signs and signals. I'd make both my thumbs and index fingers into two zeros and go "Zero Zero" to them at the counter in a slow, careful way. Then I'd make smoking sounds at them and finally I'd make off to the hotel with the Zero Zero.

LOBOTOMY

To go from Amsterdam back to Whitestone was pretty grim for a pot smoker. I would try to make up for how mundane life was in Whitestone by starting my day off with six or seven joints of Buddha Thai. When I got really frustrated, I'd go to McDonald's on Francis Lewis Boulevard to cop some coke from my friend Tony Blow, the local dealer.

For a while, I had a girlfriend in England. Her name was Jill. When I first met her, she had on a red-and-black mohair sweater and black patent-leather pants. She was very cool-looking and nice to me, but somehow I always went running back to Whitestone in terror—to be alone again. I don't know why.

The drugs and booze had taken a toll on me. They had made everything worse. My brain felt like slush. All I knew how to do was play bass in a band and be on the road. I had to tour to pay my bills. By the time the *Pleasant Dreams* album came out in 1981, I knew I'd had enough. I could see that getting high was getting me nowhere. Finally, I started going to Odyssey House in the East Village as an outpatient. It was a chance for things to get better.

I was really trying hard. I knew that I was out of shape and when I got a break from the road, I started going to the gym in College Point to lift weights. No one else who went to that gym actually needed to go there but me. It was comical. I am a ninety-pound weakling type—they were all real heavily built construction worker types. I was upsetting the vibes of the place. Finally someone started mouthing off to me and I got pissed off. I marched over to him and hit him in the gut. He was too big to hit anywhere else. He freaked. Everybody did. The place went dead silent. We were all cracking up. They couldn't believe what they had just seen. Somehow they didn't kill me, and I got away with a humble exit and a warning, "Don't ever come back here again, you creep." I was thankful for that, but I could feel myself going a bit mental.

Outside I climbed into the brand new car I had bought on credit. It was a metallic-blue Camaro with smoked-chrome mags and white-wall tires and a T-top. Most of the cars around College Point had the standard black primer color and angry roaring tires. My car was a bit flashy for the Point and I was feeling very paranoid and edgy since I was smoking lots of pot. After the incident at the gym I decided it would be better to go to an AA meeting rather than risk going home and breaking my sobriety. So, with all this mental commotion going through my head, I pulled out of my parking spot only to notice a woman pushing a baby carriage, walking right into the Camaro. I couldn't believe it. Everything went blurry and when I tried to step on the brakes I stepped on the gas pedal instead. The Camaro went berserk and I rammed it into my neighbor's van.

I got out to look at the damage. My car was fucked but I tied the hood down with some rope I had found in the garbage and I was set. I looked around to see what had happened to the woman and her baby—it didn't look like I'd hit her—so I got back in my car and somehow I backed it out of the parking space.

Then I proceeded down Bayside Boulevard to the AA meeting that was being held at a church. It was so cold that when I pulled up in front of the meeting, the car doors

LOBOTOMY

wouldn't lock because they had frozen solid. Finally, I managed to get the car locked but the keys got stuck in the lock.
By then I was really fed up and thinking of just going to the
store and buying a bottle of brandy, but I got hold of myself.
Fuck this, I thought. Nothing's going to bother me. I hadn't
taken a car out for years and was determined to enjoy myself.
I was a bit uncomfortable anyway, as I always am when I go
to a meeting and smoke, but somehow I felt sober.

Just as soon as I got to the meeting, I felt that they were
all against me. They could only criticize me. Finally I got up
from the table and began sharing, "Hello, I am Dee Dee. I
have eighty-six days clean." I could see them all cringing.
Boy, nobody gives me any credit. I was going to say something else, but instead I stormed into the kitchen to get some
cookies because I really had the munchies bad.

Eventually, the high from the joint I had smoked before
the meeting fizzled out and I sneaked out of the place only
to find the locks on my car had frozen again. After much
banging and shouting, I got inside and behind the wheel
again. But the door wouldn't shut. I stepped on the gas in
frustration and as I sped around the corner the door opened
again. Another car was coming directly at me, so I swerved
to avoid a crash. The other car took the left side door clean
off my Camaro as I scraped the paint off all the cars parked
next to the sidewalk on my right. The cops took my car away.
I guess they thought I was too out of control to drive.

Out of spite I went out and bought a three-quarter-length
car coat. Being a Ramone I was only supposed to wear
leather motorcycle jackets. I guess I should have called it

quits then, but I was really aggravated, so I dyed my hair blue-black and took to wearing a pair of Ray-Bans as a shield between me and the rest of the world. They blocked out everything, like the dope used to. Also I switched to straight black jeans that I got from Trash and Vaudeville in the Village. I was supposed to only wear ripped blue jeans in the Ramones. The way I looked at it, at least it would stop the kids in the audience from rushing the stage and grabbing the rip in my jeans and pulling it down to my ankles. I used to hate that.

John and Joey decided to lighten up on me though—at least I was trying hard not to drink and I hardly ever did coke any more. But, just as the tension between John, Joey, and me started to melt, so it became Marc Bell's turn in the spotlight. We had stopped touring to start work on the *Subterranean Jungle* album in New York. We were rehearsing at the Daily Planet, a studio on West 30th Street that I used to really like.

THINGS WEREN'T working out as planned, though. Getting ready for *Subterranean Jungle* was a rough battle. Marc was starting to flip. The years of self-abuse were catching up with him. He had that "one way ticket on the crazy train" thing going. The last stop is always off the edge. You can't come back either.

Marc was coming to rehearsals really stoned and angry. Strangely, he almost seemed happy about his condition. You couldn't win by complaining about it. He would say that he had just been to see the doctor and that it was all band-relat-

LOBOTOMY

ed. He told us that the sessions he was having with the doctor were very painful and that the doctor had put him on
dope. Then he would run out of the rehearsal room and
laugh until he calmed down a bit and returned to the studio
again for a while.

We had to be very careful around Marc, because he was
prone to violence and dangerous. No one wanted any trouble
from him. It was also funny seeing him giggling and making
strange hiccuping noises after a row with us. Sometimes it
got so bad we couldn't rehearse—Marc would drop his pants
down to his ankles, stick his bare ass in the air and start to
shake it. He would fold his arms into wings and start flapping
them up and down, as if he were trying to fly for everyone.
Finally he would peck with his nose and start running
around the room in a frenzy, shouting "Chicken beak boy!
Chicken beak boy!"

It was when we were recording on Long Island that Marc
flipped completely. I had just walked into the studio and
John and Joey were waiting for me by the door.

"Don't go in there, Dee Dee," they said.

"Ok. What's happening, dudes?" I replied.

"Go home," they told me. "It's Marc, he's flipped his wig.
He's in there now doing that chicken beak boy dance. He's
really out of control. It looks bad, Dee Dee."

I TOOK the night off. I went back to Whitestone and worried about everything. When I got to the recording studio the
next day it was a wreck. Every piece of furniture had been
overturned. All the windows in the control booth had been

140

broken and it smelled of vodka and cheap wine. There was a clean-up crew in the studio, trying to clear it up. Joey and Johnny were there, showing Billy Rogers, a session drummer from New York, a song they wanted to do. Marc wasn't there. I never found out what really happened. When I asked Johnny Ramone he glared at me hatefully and I knew something was up.

"Let's get to work, Dee Dee," he answered, as if that was an explanation of where Marc was. I could tell that I was on John's shit list again.

This sucks, I thought.

THE NEXT day I drove into Manhattan with Monte to pick up Joey and drive him to the studio. When Monte got out of the van to ring Joey's bell, I made my escape. I went down to 10th Street and First Avenue to cop. I met a dealer called Baby and I scored some coke off her. I didn't think the coke would hurt because I wasn't boozing.

I was wrong. It turned me into a paranoid schizophrenic. I became impossible to deal with. No one could trust me. I was trying to lie my way out of everything.

In an attempt to change, I tried getting help by going to Odyssey House. I also went to a private psychiatrist.

Nothing seemed to help.

I was too far gone.

Road to Ruin

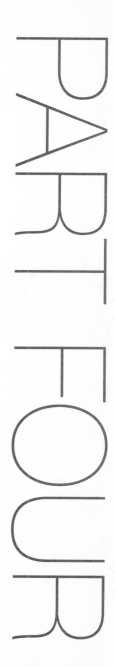

PART FOUR

One for the Road

Year after year, the Ramones traveled the world, play-

ing our music loud and fast. We were one of the best bands

that ever was. When the Ramones would come to town, it

would be magic. But no one was ever satisfied. They

always wanted more: more of this and more of that.

LOBOTOMY

Still, we kept playing. It was a way of life. We were a family, no matter what, and somehow we were more familiar with each other than with other people. We were very introverted, except for Joey. We really didn't let many people in our lives. That's why, when it was over, I was surprised to find that there was no one there.

We played with everybody. We even played with Toto! Once, in Lake Charles, Louisiana we were scheduled to play with Toto and I had just read an article that said it was one of the top ten most violent towns in America. I was worried, but it ended up being okay.

Another time, in Waterbury, Connecticut we opened for Johnny Winter. The policemen felt sorry for us, having to go out in front of that crowd and be the Ramones! We had to get off the stage in about seven minutes because the crowd got so hostile.

We opened for Ozzy, for Van Halen. I was in seventh heaven on that tour. I used to like David Lee Roth; he and I were always smoking pot together, in Spain, all over the place. We'd go find a closet and get in there and smoke and he'd tell me crazy stories. He tried to convince me he was Mexican. I believed him but he's really Jewish! He was really good at karate. He'd warm up doing karate moves.

We played with Black Flag at the Palladium. That night was a heavy night. There was a bad riot. They broke all the windows on Hollywood Boulevard. I saw policemen hitting girls with truncheons. It took about five hours just to get out of there.

There was a riot in Auckland, where they killed some

police dogs. And in Milan, we were playing a huge football stadium, and the lighting towers were shabby. There must have been 30,000 people there. Too many people climbed up onto the lighting towers and we saw them fall right over, squashing the crowd. I have a big imagination, but I am sure that that night I saw a police car just plowing through the crowd.

We played with the Runaways, and the girls came back to my hotel room and made fun of me because I was listening to Jackson Browne. "Oh, we didn't know you were like that!" they said, and just walked out on me.

I told Joan Jett and Cheri Currie, "Good, I didn't want you to be here anyway."

We toured with the Talking Heads. I got along well with them. They were fun, and they liked to smoke a lot of hash.

I did get a little jealous of them because they seemed to have more money than us. No matter how grateful you are, it's hard not to start thinking, "Why not the Ramones?"

It seemed like the whole New Wave thing was being so well represented on the radio, and that disturbed me. A lot of those bands were good, like Elvis Costello and the B-52's, but terrible bands like A Flock of Seagulls or the Cars were "radio-friendly," and sooner or later, everybody goes along with it.

Johnny Ramone could see it coming—he was the one person—because he's such a purist. He told us all the time, way back in the days of *Saturday Night Fever*, that individual freedom of expression was going to be ruined by corporate music.

LOBOTOMY

At the time, it would ruin my fun, because I like *Saturday Night Fever* and Donna Summer—and KC has written some of the best songs of all time. But Johnny was very protective and singular-versed.

Of course, today, it's come to pass. It's a sociological change in the world, and it's a conservative mentality. The bid for survival has affected everything. And it's boring and nonsexual. I would hate to be in a band like No Doubt or Green Day. It's a producer's world. The Backstreet Boys are okay, but it doesn't sound like they're trying to seduce a woman to me. They aren't Smokey Robinson.

And Britney Spears? I wouldn't go out with her. You think her mother would like me?

Hard Pressed

In the mid-eighties, the Ramones signed a three-album

deal with Beggar's Banquet in England. We had just

released the *Too Tough to Die* album and the label was

doing everything possible to promote the band. Martin

Mills, the head of Beggar's Banquet, also signed The Cult.

He wanted us to put out "Bonzo Goes To Bitburg." Johnny

LOBOTOMY

Ramone didn't like the song title and it caused a lot of problems. On our *Animal Boy* album the song is called "My Brain Is Hanging Upside Down" to please Johnny Ramone, a big Ronald Reagan fan. At least Joey and me fought for the title for the single. And for once, we won.

But for this album, Beggar's Banquet went all out for a song I wrote with Dave Stewart of the Eurythmics called "Howling at the Moon." It was about marijuana. Beggar's Banquet called Overland, our management office, and asked Joey and me to fly over to London to do press for the record. It sounded great—a good way to get away from Johnny and Marc for a while. But we knew that Monte would have to come to make sure we did our job and to baby-sit Joey and me. There wasn't much we could do about it. Monte had to be there. He was coming and that was that.

Monte had a wicked streak in him. We nicknamed him "The Detective" because he was such a snoop. He was determined that no one would ever pull the wool over his eyes. It was really a drag. He was a mass of self-pitying frustration and no fun to be with. Marc Bell gave Monte the nickname "Lambie." Our sweet Lambie. It was to drive Monte crazy on purpose. Marc would work himself up into a frenzy in the van, making lamb noises until Monte would flip. Then the Lamb would threaten to drive us off the road and he would step on the gas. He would get the wild sheep-eyed look and a beet-red face and start shouting "We're all going to perish now, you fucking creeps. We're all going to get killed, Marc, because you wouldn't shut up. You're the Lamb, Marc! You! You! You!"

Surviving the Ramones

It would get extreme. Past ninety mph, the real action would start, the real yelling. The baying lamb noises at their most joyful. I didn't have any pet names for Monte. Joey just called him "asshole." To Joey, everyone was an asshole. Joey put Monte through a lot. Maybe he should go for counseling after he stops road managing. I bet Monte has a lot to get off his chest; most rock stars are difficult. You can form resentments.

I looked on the trip to England purely as a way of tasting the good life. I was hoping that we would all stick together and make everyone jealous when we got back to New York. It's ironic that I had to escape a popular rock'n'roll band to fulfil my fantasies, but I was a mass of frustration, and by then, very desperate. I wasn't fooling around this time. I wanted my drugs, booze and a *femme fatale* to go along with them. My mind was made up. No cretin road manager was going to sabotage my fun. I was going to party, party, party. No one was going to tell me what to do. I could see from the henpecked expression on Joey's face that he was in the same boat. Why couldn't we just admit that we needed to go crazy?

By the time we all dragged ourselves to the airport, Monte was already acting the worried manager. For my part, I thought I deserved to have some fun. I was doing all this extra work for the Ramones—flying to England in February to do interviews with the creepy English press. The biggest assholes in the world. Smarty-farties, that's what we called them. So, was it any surprise that I needed to let loose? Jesus Christ, what harm was it to have a few drinks and some lines in the bathroom before a six-hour flight?

LOBOTOMY

Monte came over to me before we boarded the plane and told me to watch it, that I was probably an alcoholic. *What do they want from me?* I thought. That's why I always ended up being sneaky. Because everybody was always on my case and not minding their own business. On the plane I told Monte to fuck off. That I was pissed off, that I was almost crazy already. I told him to take a good look at himself. That I'd only had one drink that morning—a double shot of Bailey's Irish Cream with a shot of rum poured into it. I only had one double Bloody Mary on the whole six-hour flight to London. I vowed to get them all back one day for what they were putting me through. For always ruining my fun. So I marched to the rest room on the plane and stayed there for twenty minutes. I knew that Monte would start to worry that I had overdosed in the toilet or something like that. It worked. Monte was soon politely knocking on the bathroom door, just as I predicted.

"Dee Dee, everything all right in there?"

I flung the door open and snarled, "Oh yeah, sure, right. I can't even take a shit in peace. See what I mean? You're an asshole. I hate you. It's because of assholes like you that I'm an alcoholic. And if I am one, then you made me one. Nobody cares about me. I am going to quit. As soon as we get back to New York, I am going to see a lawyer and I am going to sue the Ramones and everybody, so fuck you all."

Monte wasn't phased one bit. He just pushed his frizzy-top mug into my face and made a lamb noise at me. I wish I could translate it for you, it was sort of like "baaa he hey hehey hee ha ha ha." Horrible. Monte did the "ha ha ha" directly into my ear, which left me quite distressed. At 13,000 feet a person's ears are doubly sensitive, so it was a shitty thing to do. I went meekly back to my seat.

When the plane landed at Gatwick, the customs official gave Joey the usual hard time. Then they started up with me. Well, enough is enough. So I snarled, "Why don't you guys pick on the real crooks?"

"Huh?"

"You know you guys are a right bunch of assholes, aren't you?—and gimme back my passport, motherfuckers."

Either I'd put them in their place or they were just tired and wanted to go home or something. I don't really know, I am not a psychiatrist. But they stamped on my passport "All Special Privilege" and said "Welcome to England, Mr Colvin."

"May I proceed then?" I responded.

"Yes, sir."

"Ok, then. See you next time," and I went on my way. See how easy it can be if you know how to handle yourself?

There was a driver waiting to collect us and our luggage and scoot us to the Kensington Hilton, where we were staying. We always stayed there in those days because then the pubs used to close at three o'clock in the afternoon. The Kensington Hilton had an international bar for tourists so we could drink twenty-four hours around the clock. We could also order cheeseburgers and milkshakes any time of day or night, but in those days they only had Wimpy's, so that sucked. As Americans, we thought it was important to retain certain standards while in the UK. The rooms in the London

LOBOTOMY

Kensington Hilton were a real treat—they had a booze-vending machine that shot out those little bottles like you could get on the plane.

As soon as I got to my room, I threw my luggage down and poured myself a shot of bourbon, a scotch, and then another bourbon, which I mixed with some warm Coke. Then I passed out for forty-five minutes. I was awakened by an amused Glorya Robinson from Red Eye, who handled the Ramones in England.

Glorya had been my girlfriend when I was sixteen, back in Forest Hills, and now she was living in England and had an English husband. Glorya was no saint herself, but even someone as hardened as her had some reservations about dealing with me. She was tough and quite ready for me.

"Dee Dee, you shit. Get up. Get up right now. I mean it. Someone wants to interview you. Get up, you lazy sod! I hate you!"

"Man, what a way to start the day," I thought to myself.

"Ok, Glorya," I said, "I'm almost ready. Do you have a joint?"

She knew I'd ask that. But she didn't have one. Nobody seemed to have pot in England then. Maybe some creepy black hash, but no pot. Everybody had to get by on pints of beer, speed, and cheap whiskey. So all Glorya had was a half-empty pint of booze in her purse to see her through the afternoon, so I left her alone. That's England, I thought. What a bore. Then I rolled myself out of bed, because the interviewers were starting to bang on the door. The only reason I let them in is because I was hoping they would have a joint.

Surviving the Ramones

They were just two typical beer-soaked journalists. The type that think they know everything, and are punk rock snobs who double-hate Americans because we are better at everything than limeys are. We know that, so we give them a lot of grief. The girl setting up the tape recorder was the snob. Her partner, a male, looked like a "poor" student from a rich British family. I broke the tension with a "Hey, guys, got any dope?" That seemed to do the trick. They actually had some.

"Yes, Dee Dee, we have some. Actually it's quite lovely."

"Is it speed?"

"Oh yes, and it's quite nice."

So they sprinkled me a few lines and soon I was feeling very sorry for myself, but also happy because I had an excuse to justify some outrageous behavior. But first I had to be interviewed.

"Dee Dee, how did the Ramones influence the Sex Pistols?"

"I don't know. Who cares? Why do you want to start trouble by asking me a question like that right at the start? You're creeps. Get out. Get out now."

So they went on to the next question.

"Dee Dee, what did you think of the British punk bands?"

I went blank. I was so confused and feeling so dishonest that I was really getting annoyed.

"Get out. Get out now," I protested. "Ok, Johnny Moped was all right. I like him and The Damned, and X-Ray Spex are alright as well."

"What is your favorite British band then, Dee Dee?" the snob interrupted me.

"Eddie and the Hod Rods. So fuck off mate. Get out. Get out now. I am sick of all this."

"But Dee Dee, what about the Bay City Rollers?"

"Oh, hold on a minute. Now you're talking my language. 'Saturday Night,' best new-wave song ever, mate. So fuck off."

"Hey, how about some more speed?"

The room seemed to take on a lime-green hue as the short English afternoon started turning into a gloomy English evening. Speed. Crummy, crummy speed. It makes you crazy.

After a while, the snob and the student left. More interviewers kept coming in and out of the room. We emptied the minibar three times in three hours and called room service for beer and Cokes. I was in top form, but very sloppy.

"Anneeey bodieee gotta joint, ta . . ." Somebody promised one. "I want it. I want it now, aaah."

Then I got bored so I suggested we go meet Martin Mills, and his pals at the Korean restaurant downstairs and ditch the journalists. I excused myself and when the coast was clear, Glorya and I sneaked into the elevator and rode down to the lobby. We didn't even bother to kick everybody out of the room.

"Martin's paying," Glorya told me. "Don't worry, Dee Dee. Those journalists are just the smarty-farties. There's nothing anyone can really do for them, but use them for what they are."

The press people were lingering downstairs in the lobby when we got there. Somehow they had beat us downstairs. We didn't even try to pretend to be polite. It was too late. The war had started so we just snob-marched past them into the restaurant where Martin and his pals were waiting. I don't remember anything about dinner—I immediately passed out on my garlic steak. Nobody wanted to talk to me because I was so smelly from sleeping face down in a bunch of chopped-up garlic. I woke up alone, by myself, at six o'clock in the morning. I had nothing to smoke. I was miserable. I wished I was back in Whitestone smoking some Thai and listening to LIR. Fuck this, I thought to myself.

I was paranoid from all the booze and speed, but the Kensington Hilton Hotel always has a good breakfast in the morning, a treat that I looked forward to. But, in my condition, I felt like I was walking through a minefield and stepping on low-self-esteem bombs that blew apart the guilt in my brain. In short, I was killing myself.

Somehow I went for breakfast. I don't know how I made it. I could barely stand up. There was pus dripping out of my eyes and my nose was dripping blood. I went back up to my room in shame, hoping no one would see me, but the hotel had those damn computer-card keys. I ended up making so much noise trying to get into my room that I woke up Monte. It was then about seven-thirty. Monte had just gone to bed. But he was glad to see me.

"Dee Dee," he said, "thank God you're here. I can't remember much of last night. I was worried anyway. You know how things can be, and . . . and . . . and . . ."

He had a lampshade on his head. A fluffy rabbit tail was glued to his underpants. He was still stinking drunk and his nostrils were coated with a white powder, which I could only guess to be drugs. I heard a young female voice call him back into the room. She sounded French. "Montee, Montee, Babeee . . ."

Monte excused himself like a gentleman and then slammed the door in my face. What a hypocrite, I thought. I wonder what his excuse is. Is it me? Right. What about Monte's secret behavior behind closed doors in the privacy of his hotel room? Well, I'm going to stop right now. I don't want to be the big baby of the Ramones, so I won't tell on him. All I had on my mind was to get away from Monte, and getting a couple of hours of sleep until I could call the porter and have the liquor machine in my room filled up again. Soon eleven o'clock rolled around and Glorya stumbled into my room. She was trying to maintain a professional approach, trying to be sweet. It didn't matter. I was still up. I'm a pro. The interviews with the BBC, *Melody Maker*, *New Musical Express*, *Sounds*—it was a lot, and Glorya was paranoid that I wouldn't do it. I was a wreck. When I saw Monte and Joey later, I could tell they were wrecks too. We were all pretty fucked up.

"We're losers, guys," I said. "Look at us. We're pathetic. Joey, just look at yourself, you're still as drunk as a skunk. It's only midday. Monte, it looks like you had another blackout. Do you want me to go over your antics last night? And . . . and . . . and . . ." I was shaking so much I couldn't continue. "Christ, I need a beer. Christ man, we all do."

Everyone was in definite agreement. Monte went over to the machine to shoot out some Cokes and scotch. He was shaking as well. I knew I had to take control, so I called room service for beer and coffee.

Surviving the Ramones

"Everything will be ok, guys," I said.

Glorya signed the bill "Martin Mills, Beggar's Banquet." It was a pretty heavy bill. Still, I knew I'd have to pay for it all in the end. Everybody knows that. Here today, gone tomorrow. That's how it is. We all know the score. We'd been around long enough by then to know to take what we could, while we could get it. Just get these interviews over with as fast as we can—skip as many as possible. The record won't sell, anyway. Let's have some fun.

So we did the interviews quick and then went back to the Korean restaurant downstairs. Tonight was party night. Hip, hip, hooray! Right on! Party, party, party! Embassy night.

"Glorya," I said. "Cancel all the fanzines first, ok?"

I just can't handle interviews. They really suck. It's always like a confrontational situation, putting me on the defensive. Then I end up flipping out and yelling, "Get out! Get out!"

I saw Jeffrey Lee Pierce from the Gun Club flip once when we played on the bill with him in a small town somewhere in southern France. He was being interviewed by some French smarty-farties and all of a sudden he flipped. The next thing you knew he was holding his white Fender Strat over his head in the battle-axe position and shouting, "Get out! Get out, you dirty French bastards and don't ever come back!"

This was much like the time I remember Johnny Ramone holding his Mosrite in the battle-axe position and shouting "Get out! Get out!" at Malcom McLaren in the Whisky a Go Go dressing room. I could go on and on. But it seems, back in the Korean restaurant, I had pulled my pants down, got up on the dinner table and tried to do the chicken beak boy dance like I had seen Marc Bell do so many times before. It was seven in the morning.

I went up to my room and had a five hour speed party to get in the right mood for the Embassy. The Embassy wasn't even that special. Girls were too hard to pick up there, then you went home by yourself. Stoned. The best thing about it was that it stayed open so late that you didn't have to go home. It would be fun, but not real fun. The fun would center around the bar and getting stoned in the bathroom.

Can you imagine trying to put me into a taxi and getting me home after a night out? It could get very, very complicated. It's easy to get stranded in London. Cabs won't pick you up. Especially if you're American and very drunk. The drivers outside the Hilton are ok. They will give you a ride, but they speed and talk too much. I guess they meet too many musicians at the hotel. At six in the morning outside the Embassy it would be nice to see them, but you won't. I was already wise to this, and I was sick of it. These guys ain't going to make my life more difficult and get away with it. No way. Something so simple as hailing a cab can be a nightmare for someone like me, though, so it's always good to have a few beer bottles with you, late night in London, to fling at the cabs. They become the enemy.

I could have had real fun, but I didn't know how. I could have gone shopping for clothes at Kensington Market, but I didn't do that until after I left the band. I could have tried to meet a girl, but I was too fucked up to care. But mostly it was about being miserable back at the hotel. That's what i remember the most—being hungover in my room. Coming down. Having nothing to do. The no-fun stuff. I hated myself and the narrow world I was living in. There was no way out of it. There was nowhere else as safe to go as what was destroying me. My life felt as empty as the trail of beer cans I left behind me wherever I went.

It was catching up with me. I was heading for a breakdown. I don't know how anybody dealt with me. Everybody was becoming the enemy. I was pissed off at everybody. Everyone hated my guts. I hated touring. It was such a boring way to live that any excitement—like just getting away from the other guys for a few days—was a big kick.

It was driving me off the rails. A "you're not going to make it out alive" type of panic started gripping me. As I made my way back to the hotel in the early morning I could tell I was in trouble. It was just too obvious, like the burning sky over Berlin after a bomb raid during World War II. I could tell something horrible was going to happen, like seeing Kessie the family dachshund drowning in the Wansee in Berlin, while my drunken father just stood there and did nothing. I knew I was in trouble. It wasn't a good feeling.

I went up to my room to pack and get ready for the plane ride back to New York. I was already feeling very sorry for myself, sorry for my sins. Sorry for Kessie, my dachshund, that I had let down. The guilt was terrible.

I tried to fortify my nerves by filling a half-full Coca-Cola can with bourbon. This is nice, I thought to myself, it's like cough medicine. In the taxi to Heathrow Airport, I made another one for myself to get me through boarding and getting to my seat, until the bar finally opened.

LOBOTOMY

When we were eventually in the air, the stewardess took my order. I ordered four little bottles of rum and two cans of Coke. She was good about it, but I do remember her laughing as she placed my drinks on the tray on the armrest.

"You're not going to be any trouble, are you sir?" she asked me.

"Oh, no" I replied. "I am just going to have these drinks and then pass out. Wake me up in New York, ok?"

I'm sure she was thinking, "Oh, all right, Yank, everything seems to be in order."

As she wiggled down the aisle toward the rear of the plane, I turned my head to get a quick look at her ass. Very quickly, so as not to bring attention to myself, I twisted open one of the rum bottles and drank it in one gulp. I then twisted the other bottle open and drank that as well. I poured the other two rums into the Coke can I had just opened and drank half of it. By the time I finished the other half of the can with the rum in it, I actually did pass out for four hours.

As soon as I woke up I knew I needed a drink.

"Oh, stewardess, I need a little drink, please!"

"I'm sorry, the bar is closed. We're landing in half an hour."

"What do you mean? Just give me a quick one. It's no big deal is it? Really, I'll give you five hundred dollars! Look, here's the money!" I said, pushing a wad of dollars at her. But she backed off.

"Fasten your seat belt," she said, staring at me as she marched backward toward the rear.

The plane had just started bucking like a maniac. It flipped her and she ended up rolling down the aisle like a bowling ball, knocking the other three stewardesses over into the passengers' seats. One busted into the toilet, breaking the door open and revealing Monte Melnick, who had been in there taking a big shit. He was stinking drunk. He didn't know what the hell was going on.

I was glad for all the chaos, as I was going to use the diversion to steal some liquor from the drinks trolley. Somehow the plane lurched violently and bucked two or three times very severely. The third time it did so, the trolley went flying down the aisle and may well have burst through the emergency door, flown out into the cold, black sky, and fallen three thousand feet into the frozen ocean below, for all I knew or cared.

I gave up all hope right then of getting a drink. My brain was buzzing like there were hornets in my head. I was going into the DT's, withdrawing from alcohol. I really needed a drink very badly, but I knew I was not going to get one. My body started preparing to go out of control. Then they made an announcement, "Attention, we are going to circle JFK for three hours because there is a lot of winter traffic tonight and we can't get permission to land." I freaked right there in my seat. I had a breakdown. I couldn't believe what I had just heard. I really could have used some Thorazine.

After an hour I was really in bad shape. The plane was shaking up and down, hitting air pockets and diving, then doing straight up climbs to avoid disaster. It kept going round and round in circles. I was contemplating suicide. I thought about jumping out of the emergency exit in a parachute. Somehow, I was trying to hide my breakdown from the other

LOBOTOMY

passengers and the stewardesses, but I think they could tell. Everything was coming apart at the seams.

"NNNooo!" I screamed over and over in my head, as they announced that we were flying over to the Hartford, Connecticut airport to land and refuel, and wait for permission to fly back to JFK to land.

"NNNooo! NNNooo! Not me! Please! No, this can't be happening to me!"

"Ladies and gentlemen," they announced a second time, "we are now flying to Hartford. Please fasten your seat belts."

"NNNooo! Not me!" I had been rummaging around behind the pillows in my seat and in the pocket in front of me, where people normally put their empty bottles of booze on the trans-Atlantic flights. I was looking for a bottle with a few last drops of booze left in it. All I found was the aluminum flap from one of the Coke cans. I twirled it around in my hand between my finger and thumb. It felt sharp. I wondered if I could go into the bathroom and use it like a razor blade to cut my wrists and finish my miserable life once and for all.

I started dreaming that if we would just land I could get to one of those Korean grocery stores on Third Avenue and get a six-pack of beer, but soon I was forgetting that idea. The thought of getting anything more to drink didn't seem to be a possibility any more. What mattered most was to hold on to my sanity. I was going over and over my explanations and excuses in case I flipped out.

I flipped out.

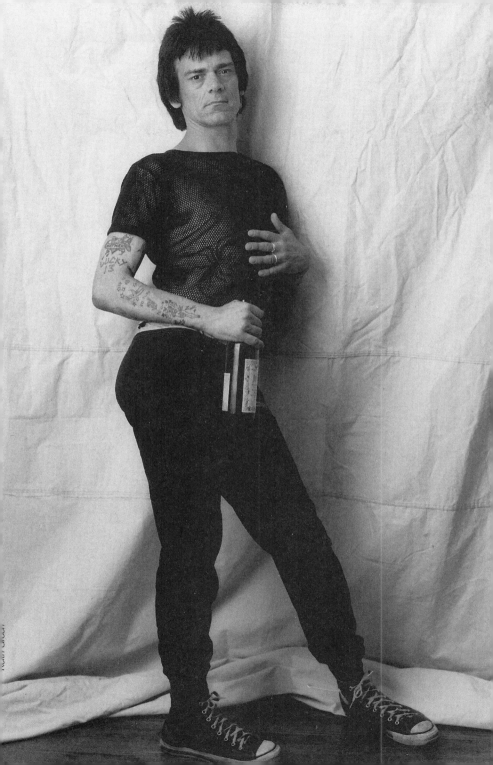

Psycho Therapy

When I got home to Whitestone—the plane had

eventually landed in Newark, New Jersey, instead of JFK

Airport—I was really in a bad way. I was convinced I was

hearing classical music. I turned the stereo on and off. No,

it wasn't coming from the stereo. I listened to the phone.

No, not the phone. The TV set? No, there was no sound

LOBOTOMY

coming from the TV. I checked everything. In my craziness, I listened to the electric socket to see if "they" were broadcasting. I couldn't find where the music was coming from. It got louder and louder.

I decided to try to take a hot bath to calm myself down. When I sat in the water, it started getting real wavy. It was weird, like sitting in the ocean, not a bathtub. I had closed the glass shower doors around the bathtub to keep the steam in. Then, all of a sudden, the glass doors exploded and the glass shattered in hundreds of tiny jagged pieces. It was freaky. Whatever force it was that broke those shower doors, it wasn't subtle. The explosion was wicked, but none of the glass stuck into me or cut me. Why, I don't know, but I still got the point. Glass had filled up the bottom of the bathtub like sand in the bottom of a bucket.

I jumped right out of the bathtub. I knew that this was a message to me from the underworld, a greeting from hell. I was really paranoid by now. Twenty minutes later I was on the phone, "Hello, this is Dee Dee Ramone. I am going crazy. Send an ambulance. I am flipping out beyond return. I mean it! No-hope crazy, ok? Berserk, completely insane!"

But after I had called 911, I called Tony Blow, my coke dealer. "Hello, Tony, it's Dee Dee. Can you deliver right away? It's urgent." He came over and I got some coke from him and snorted it up. I did it as fast as humanly possible, since I was so used to doing it on the sneak anyway. Then all of a sudden the police and paramedics walked into my living room out of nowhere. Christ, I thought, I'm busted. But the detective was cheerful. I was stunned.

"Dee Dee, my friend," he said, "How would you like to go downtown?" This was about the fifth time that I had been taken away.

I didn't know what to think, but as I put two and two together, I figured that this might be my ride out of Whitestone. I needed to get to the city again to cop some more cocaine. I was coming apart at the seams. All I could think of was more coke, more coke, more coke . . .

"Detective, sir," I said, trying to seem cheerful, "Do you think we could swing by the East Village for a minute?"

"Why not, Dee Dee?" the detective said. "That's a great idea."

It's a miracle, I thought.

"I am ready now, let's go!" I said to him, and we headed out the door to the police van.

I started going over a plan. As soon as we got near 10th Street in the East Village, I would jump out of the van and escape. I figured I could get the jump on the cop until he pulled over and ran after me. I planned to get to Baby, cop the blow and do it all in one toot, so the police couldn't take it away. I knew already that they would catch me again right away, but what could I do? I was doing my best.

The cop was tricky, though. He got the jump on me faster than normal. He was actually in the process of kidnapping me. Going to the East Village to 10th Street and all that was just a diversionary tactic that the cop was getting me to play up to, so that I would be more manageable. In fact, the detective was actually trying to be nice about everything and get me to a hospital before I flipped out completely. He had

LOBOTOMY

alerted the staff at Gracie Square that he was bringing me in, so everybody was waiting on the street for me.

I can usually find my way around in Manhattan, but this time I was so stoned that I didn't know where I was. I was flipping. I had had about as much as I could take. I panicked, and in my confused state, I suddenly flung open the door on my side of the van and ran like a wild man down the sidewalk.

The thing is, though, that I wasn't downtown, I was right in front of Gracie Square, and Dr. Finkel, who had taken over my case from Dr. Hanch at Odyssey House, was there waiting for them to bring me in. He spotted me immediately. He was obviously expecting me to be difficult and had his personal hospital assistants positioned strategically on the block. They caught me fairly easily—I was very out of shape and near a complete breakdown by then. They put me in a restraining device and gave me a massive dose of Thorazine to calm me down. After they wrestled me into the building and into the elevator, Dr. Finkel took out his stethoscope and notepad and looked me over. After three minutes, the required legal minimum for observation, he declared me totally insane and put me in the quiet room for the night.

All I can remember about the rest of what happened is that I woke up the next day in the rubber room at Gracie Square, a well-known institution in New York. It was sort of like that place in the Ramones "Psycho Therapy" video. It was real scary. I am used to the worst, but this was the absolute pits. Being surrounded by a bunch of maniacs was too much for me. I started feeling very confused and sorry for myself. I had no idea where I was, if it was Manhattan, Queens, or even California. I knew I was locked up, but not in jail. I was in some kind of a deep fog.

The rubber room. It was insane. I was freaking out at first, but then I sunk into a hopeless valley of depression and went blank. Everybody had a green gown with slippers which had that yellow happy face on them. I guess when you're nodding from the Thorazine and your head begins to fall, you were supposed to see that face and cheer up. I had that same vacant look on my face like everyone else did, and we were all looking at each other.

When trouble started, it was usually because someone was looking at someone else the wrong way. To this day I flip if someone looks at me the wrong way. Finally, I started coming down and they put me in the regular population. I was given a room to share with a negro. He was quiet and well-behaved. He just lay on his cot, sleeping with his eyes open, and I sat in the window frame looking at a light bulb.

I was snapping out of it, but then they moved a Spanish guy in on us who was a crack addict with shredded lungs. He would twist and turn all night. His teeth would be chattering and his lungs wheezing. Finally he would pass out for an hour or two and start snoring. The noise became so threatening and disturbing that Dr. Finkel decided to put me in a room with some guys who were less hopelessly damaged and more settled into the hospital. The idea was that I could pull myself together and settle my nerves. They put me in with a huge black guy called Tree Top and an overweight, swishy Spanish queen. Tree Top was as strong as an oak, but a good person and not violent at all. The queen drove me berserk. He talked all day long about his oversexed mother and his childhood in the Bronx, and about a place he used to go called the Indian Rock.

I was the oldest one there, the only dope fiend, and the only one who had never done crack. I couldn't relate to this new breed of addicts. It was spooky. Can you imagine how Tree Top and that queen were pushing my buttons? They were in great spirits and delighted to have me there. They were planning our future together and were determined that we would hang out together when they let us go. The queen wanted to take me to some park in the Bronx to show me the Indian Rock. I was flipping. I hadn't had any sleep for five days. They made me go to classes and AA meetings all day, and then put me in a dual-focus group. I had to do something, so I started hiding in the space between my bed and the wall, so no one could find me and I wouldn't have to go anywhere.

Tree Top was a little stupid, though, and he wouldn't leave the room unless I would go with him. Finally I would just hop into the crack between my bed and the wall. Tree Top would start losing it then. His eyes would get wilder and more paranoid by the second. Anybody could tell that I was hiding where I was, because he was making it so obvious that something was up. When Dr. Finkel came into the room to see what was going on, he would shout, "Tree Top, where's Douglas?" and Tree Top would point to where I was and say, "He's there." That was fucked up. They also made me play volleyball. It was a nightmare.

Surviving the Ramones

Finally, Tree Top's snoring and the queens's babbling drove me over the edge. It was the fifth day, four in the morning, and I had finally gone insane. I overturned a trash can and started banging it with a Coca-Cola can.

"Good morning, motherfuckers! Good morning, fucking asshole creeps. Good morning, did you hear me? I am getting the hell out of here! You guys have driven me berserk. Are you happy now?"

Then I froze. The hurt look on the queen's ugly mug was so sorrowful. Tree Top was terrified and hiding between his bed and the space between the wall. I've seen it all, I thought to myself. I can't take any more of this. I just shut up. The vibes were terrible. We were all drained. I grabbed a shopping bag and a black plastic Hefty bag and started packing up my stuff.

"Bye, bye, assholes!" I shouted, and then started struggling out the door and into the hallway.

"Where you going?" Tree Top hollered. I was stalling anyway, so I took advantage of the grace of the moment.

"I'm gettin' outta here! I'm going!"

"Oh, Dee Dee, darling!" the queen said, daring me to make one more move. "If you make a fuss around here, they'll put you in a restraining device and throw you in the rubber room."

"Even if I just wanna leave?" I said, feeling a bit defeated.

"Jesus Christ!" Tree Top said. "You can't just leave here when you want to, man! This is a mental institution! You lost all human rights when they locked you in this joint. So shut the fuck up!"

LOBOTOMY

"No way. I'm going."

I was real shaky, though, and I didn't want to go back to the rubber room. I felt myself coming apart at the seams again, and then Dr. Finkel walked into the room. He had been working around the clock for five days straight, and hadn't been home yet, and hadn't shaved for five days. I checked his beard out and thought to myself, *He looks like a Marxist revolutionary*. I calmed down right away, and decided not to shave any more either. That will drive them crazy, I thought. Even Johnny Ramone told me once that the ultimate was to shave your head and grow a beard. Which, by the way, I have done.

While I was digesting all this information, Tree Top and the queen were holding their breath. I was going blank and Dr. Finkel was about to lose his cool, so I broke the ice.

"We're not doing nothing!"

"Well, what's all the commotion about, Douglas?"

"Oh, nothing."

"Well then, you guys get some sleep now! Tomorrow is going to be a long day."

They let me out of there two weeks later. When I walked back into my apartment in Whitestone I had a beard. The beard really flipped everyone out. Johnny Ramone was really against it. For the next five years I fought for my right to have a beard. I used the fact that every one of my psychiatrists had one. Sometimes I'd give in and shave it off. Then I'd grow it again. I made myself a promise that some day I would be able to do as I wanted. Like Fidel Castro, Dr. Finkel, the guys in ZZ Top, or the guy on the rolling papers that I used to smoke marijuana, I saw a beard as the reward you earn by being a successful outlaw type like me. It means, "Stay away, don't fuck with me. I am mean. Get off my case, mother-fuckers."

Dee Dee and Nina Hagen in Germany, 1995.
Barbara Zampini

By the time the Ramones were touring South America,

the last thing I needed was any more cocaine in my sys-

tem, but I was greedy and that's where the stuff comes

from. When we finally landed in Buenos Aires, which was

the last city on this particular tour, I was really ill. I was

crashing and very demoralized. After I made it through

customs, I wandered off from the band, who were making small talk with the local groupies. I had tried to get marijuana in every city in South America, but never had any luck. It was hard to get. I was freaking out by the time I got to Argentina, so I sneaked away from everyone to try to score some weed somewhere in the airport. I chanced upon a Latin American gentleman who said he could help me. We went to the parking lot together, and he had weed in the trunk of his car. It was a fancy car—he was obviously some kind of successful survivor–type.

So we hit it off. I got into his car and he drove me to the hotel. He said he could have all the cocaine he wanted, but he wasn't interested. He had lived in the jungle with the Indians on a coca-paste camp. He said that he was smoking massive amounts of cocaine a day before he hit bottom. Then he had to pull himself slowly back to sanity. He said that the drugs really did a number on him—that with drugs, you couldn't win.

"Dee Dee," he told me, "It is common knowledge that Che Guevara ran dope into the United States to fuck up American society."

Whenever I toured South America with the Ramones, I came home a mess. Before I left I always had high hopes that it would be the "Big One." In Whitestone, about the most excitement I got was watching the girls in the ZZ Top videos on MTV. I was eager to get to Rio, the city that boasts the world's most beautiful women. Everyone else felt the same way, but we were also trying to keep our home lives calm. When Monte came to pick me up, I tried to act miserable, and said a meek goodbye to Mr. Smith, my pet parrot, so as not to upset him. Monte scooted me out the door and into the van. As soon as we were on the Brooklyn-Queens Expressway, I let out a "Hip Hip Hooray!" and lit up a joint. I was dreaming about topless beaches, girls, and cocaine.

"Forget it, Dee Dee," Monte said. He could see trouble. "We're only going to São Paulo and Buenos Aires. Rio is too much of a party town. So, I told the promoter not to book us there."

I couldn't believe him. Monte seemed like he might get really difficult this time. I tried to play innocent to keep him level. After all, he was driving. He had threatened to drive the van off the road in the past when he was stressed, and I believed that one day he would actually do it. I just wanted to be partying in South America, far away from Whitestone.

When we got to the airport, I saw Joey and everybody standing around waiting to board the plane. You could tell right away that they were trying to hide something, trying to look inconspicuous, but it was an act. I was acting as well. We were trying to keep up a professional front, but flashed each other secret smirks, suggesting sin and debauchery, to keep up our courage. Everybody played the game and behaved themselves on the flight. We cleared customs with no trouble, then we went to our rooms in the hotel in São Paulo and there was nothing to do. I was full of anxiety, but I thought, this place isn't so bad.

I had previously placed my order for cocaine, and someone was supposed to score for me while I waited in my room at the hotel for them. They were taking their sweet time and I had had enough. I was about to flip.

LOBOTOMY

"Motherfuckers! Cocksuckers! I hate everybody's guts! Are you happy now? Is this what you want?"

I had been there five hours already, and all I was getting was the old runaround. I had never felt so mean in my life. Here was my one chance to do cocaine in South America, and life plays another sick joke on me. I'd heard from everyone I asked that everybody has it. It's excellent. You can get it everywhere, that it's ten dollars a gram, the purest rocks around. Well, why didn't I have any then? Typical. They didn't get us any marijuana either. It was a nightmare. I waited up all night for the phone to ring, but no one called or came by my room. Finally we let a fan come backstage after our show. Normally we wouldn't do that, but I was desperate. I had to sit there and make small talk with him while he took forever to roll a spliff, which was 90 percent rolling paper, tobacco, and such a small piece of black hash that I didn't even get a buzz.

I was hoping for a party when we got back to the hotel, and I wasn't disappointed. It was pretty lively. The show had been a big success, and there was a bunch of hot Latin babes prowling around in the shortest miniskirts I have ever seen. They were offering themselves to us and trying to get in the elevator with us to come to our rooms.

At the bar in the lobby of the hotel, the elite of the Brazilian underground night creatures were hanging out and waiting for us. The hotel guests were hanging out at the bar and in the lobby, and everyone was real, real stoned. There was no pretense of being goody-goody types. That went out the window right away. It was great. What a night!

Surviving the Ramones

They had a doctor to dispense cocaine to the lucky few. It was supposed to be the ultimate to get coke from him. He had a little black medicine bag and a white doctor's uniform on. He made us all feel better. I was having the time of my life, riding the elevators up and down and making faces at people, running up and down the halls, yelling.

My little folly turned sour around eight in the morning in the hotel lobby coffeeshop. I was sitting there alone, very demoralized, and crashing. I ordered a few beers and tried to eat breakfast, to try and pull myself together, but my hangover was starting to overpower me, and I still had to pack my suitcase, I had a flight to catch in an hour.

It was a treadmill, going nowhere, and it was hell once I

realized it. I said to myself, "I hate these people, I'm not

growing, I'm not learning anything. This is an act."

There was no way to just take it as a job, even through

we were lucky to be making an income. They'd program

you to fight for the big, big thing so that we couldn't realize that we were already somewhat successful. We were just hoping for more, more, more. We weren't successful to ourselves. We hadn't had that big-selling album to match the Clash's or the other bands that had albums go platinum. We weren't even going gold. Slowly but surely, we were turning into a club band, and the rest of the members resented me for it. They wouldn't give me the time of day.

I didn't like sitting up there in the front of the van and making small talk about things that bored me to death, like baseball. And I didn't need to listen to the new Van Halen record or the new Foreigner record. Or the new Alice Cooper record. I mean, Alice was great but in 1984, come on.

It starts to wear you out. You're in the airport, and you're just there, there's nothing to do. Maybe four people come over and ask you for your autograph. And then two hundred people just amuse themselves by staring at you. I always hated signing autographs and meeting fans and trying to sell the Ramones. I remember when Henry Rollins wrote about hiding from fans in the van on tour with Black Flag I could relate.

And people are always trying to give you advice. "I didn't like that article about you, I don't like this song. I don't like that kind of criticism." Meanwhile, other people are always betraying your privacy or exaggerating things about you just to gain notoriety, always talking about things from your personal past.

Joey started drinking seriously. It seemed that as soon as I started to consider quitting drinking, he started up. We'd have to go pick him up at a bar called Paul's on 10th Street and drag him to the recording studio. And he was constantly yelling at me. "I'm not afraid of you Dee Dee," he'd yell.

There were periods when Joey was a perfect person on the road. But one of the reasons I considered stopping doing cocaine was because he reminded me of myself. I saw how ugly it got, when people came to your room at four, five, and six in the morning looking for another line. "Dee Dee, you got a line? You got any lines?"

"I don't know," I'd say, trying to sleep. "Ask Arturo, he's probably got some."

And then they'd start bickering with me. "No, I know you got some."

Wherever we'd go we'd hear stories about Joey: He broke his nose falling over a drum set at a party, he got too drunk and locked himself in the bathroom to get high.

We had trouble making some dates in California, and our opening act, Murphy's Law, was furious. They had to sit around and wait for us. And there was a rumor that Johnny Ramone told the promoter, Premiere, not to book them in any other shows so they wouldn't compete with attendance when we finally did get there. One of the guys in Murphy's Law freaked out and threatened Johnny; it was a mess.

We finally got to California and we'd booked an early show at the Roxy at four in the afternoon. We were staying at the Holiday Inn on Highland. And I got up really early in the morning, like I always do, to go across the street and get some doughnuts, coffee, and the paper. It was seven in the morning.

Joey was just getting back to the hotel. He had been partying all night long. He had a bottle of champagne in one

LOBOTOMY

hand and some fat horrible girl in a miniskirt with him. Our show was lousy and everybody was upset.

"Can he sing? Will he be able to sing?" That was the constant worry.

When we got back to New York there were a lot of

rumors flying around. Everyone was in trouble. We went

right into the studio to work on the *Animal Boy* album, and

there was more commotion than usual. Matt Lolya, one of

the road crew, showed up at the studio with his stuff in a

black-plastic Hefty bag and a shopping bag from some

supermarket in Brooklyn. His old lady had thrown him out. It was a strange way to record an album.

When we were laying down the tracks for a song called "Love Kills" about Sid Vicious, I was so nervous that I couldn't play the bass part and John had to do it. I excused myself and went to the bathroom and poured myself a drink from the bottle of wine that I had hidden between the trash can and the plastic liner bag. Then I went back into the studio to argue with everybody, but by then it didn't matter. I was having severe chest pains, so we had to end early.

This ain't so bad, I thought to myself. Since we'd ended early, I figured I could sneak over to 10th Street to see Baby and cop some coke. I decided I would go to see my doctor the next day about the pains in my chest. If I was going to have a heart attack, there was no way I was going to sing "Wart Hog" when we played New Haven the next day. They made me sing it anyway. I tried to stick up for myself, but the Ramones were very stubborn—they always won.

Except for once, somewhere in the Catskills at a Jewish resort in upstate New York, when I decided to get sneaky on them and play the helpless heart attack schtick that I had learned from the *Sanford and Son* show on TV. I started moaning and shifting about in the back of the van, like I imagined Fred Sanford would have done.

I started up with them, claiming that they were driving me to an early grave. I started whining that I would have a heart attack if I had to sing "Wart Hog" again. Eventually I wore them out, and they agreed to work out a deal with me to keep the peace. I still wasn't satisfied and kept up my spiel until I

Surviving the Ramones

was in a frenzy. I insisted that Monte pull over and dial 911 and get me an ambulance. Finally, Monte pulled over and flagged down a cop car. I jumped out of the van and started running for my life. Because of my weak heart, the cops caught me pretty easily, and I spent the night under observation. I hate strange hospitals and would rather have sung "Wart Hog," but I had gone too far again. And, as usual, I had to pay the price.

By this stage, Johnny Ramone decided everything for the Ramones. I sat in the back of the van and they sat up front. No one ever spoke to me. John and Joey had a few phoney conversations, but that was about it. I don't know if everyone wanted to listen to the baseball game all day, but Monte would never turn it off because John wanted it that way.

By 1985 I was starting to have more imaginary heart attacks. But instead of going to a psychiatrist, I insisted on going to every cardiologist in Queens and Long Island. They put me in a long tube and took X-rays of me. It was like a Frankenstein experiment; I loved it and it made me feel very special. Usually I would wake up at six o'clock in the morning, hold my heart and call the paramedics. They didn't have any sympathy for me, however, so I would just get up.

It was my favorite time of day. I would put on a strong cup of coffee, roll up six or seven joints of Buddha Thai and I'd dream myself out of Whitestone. By then I was having a lot of escape fantasies about jobs I could do to support myself, so I could quit the Ramones. Like being a doorman, or a candy-store owner, or having a hot dog stand. I was serious. I'd had enough.

LOBOTOMY

One of the best Ramones escape fantasies I had was around this time. The band was driving home from Boston. It was about six in the morning and we got to one of those toll booths in Connecticut. All the delivery trucks were lined up along the highway. The orange sun was warming up the oil and gasoline on the concrete. It all seemed very glorious to me. There were the trucks that delivered the morning papers to Queens. Then there were the bread and milk trucks that delivered to little grocery stores. It all seemed so friendly.

I've been driving this route between Boston and New York for seventeen years now, I thought, as I took another deep drag of Thai weed. The Thai was really strong and helped me escape into a deep fantasy—I was going to buy a Wonder-Bread delivery truck to take bread to supermarkets in Queens. Suffice to say, I just kept playing bass for the "brudders." It was real crummy.

What happened next was awful. I accepted a line of cocaine in the bathroom of the Whitestone Church at an AA meeting. Then I ended up sneaking over to Francis Lewis Boulevard to cop a gram of coke from Tony Blow. That really set me back. For about six months I became cocaine crazy.

One day I went to pick up Joey at his building on 9th

Street and I passed a strip where girls would work, around

12th Street. Sometimes it would take a long time, waiting

for Joey, so we'd all get out of the van and hang around, go

to Trash and Vaudeville, buy some clothes, whatever.

LOBOTOMY

One time I saw Connie there, turning tricks, trying to get dope.

Then I saw her again, and again. After we broke up, she was stalking me, and I had had to leave town. She wouldn't let go. After I had moved back to New York, I didn't really know what had happened to her.

Once I had written her from the road. Another time, she called me and told me she was at Berstein's, a detox center; I think it was on 15th Street and 2nd Avenue. She told me to walk by, and wave, because she was being held, locked up. So I did that, but we never spoke.

Now she was working the streets, and she looked skinny, and bad. I tried running after her but she would always run away. I tried to talk to her, give her some money so she wouldn't have to work, so she could get high. But she would just take off. She didn't want to associate with anyone.

Then I was in Toronto and John called me. He said, "Did you hear Tommy died?"

And I said, "Tommy?"

And he said, "No, Connie." I had misheard him. Connie had overdosed. It was as bad as you can imagine.

I said, "Oh." That's all I said to show any emotions about anything. I didn't dare. I kept everything quiet and I never really talked to too many people.

STILL, I started not wanting to die. I started saying, "I want to live." I started to become afraid of death; before, I never really cared.

Surviving the Ramones

I tried to do a lot of things differently. I even tried to take piano lessons once. The teacher had to get me a children's piano manual. But I couldn't learn, I was hopeless.

And it took me a long time to become myself. I wish I could have known that I didn't have to always hide myself. That myself was good enough.

I wish I could have changed the times, all the times I walked around, thinking that there was something wrong with me. I wish I would have been able to say *Wow, Dee Dee, you're really accomplishing a lot*, instead of always taking the negative approach. I wish I could have dealt with reality on reality's terms. I think I might have gotten more out of life had I just seen what was right there in front of me.

I hurt people. Once, back in '77, I had a fight in an apartment, a bad one. I threw the guy into one of those folding closets, and knocked him down. And I was kicking him and kicking him and kicking him, trying to finish him off. He was also drunk. And he started saying something. He knew who I was, but he started crying, "No, Daddy, no no no!"

He was hurt. Why couldn't I have just said, "Fuck you!" and ran out? I felt defenseless, and I had to make sure that I couldn't be pushed around. The paranoia and the street fights really ruined my life. And I never wanted to go back there.

I always ruined everything. Once there was a nice dinner for me in London. I was going to meet my idol, Davy Dee from Dave Dee Dosey Beak and Tish. They were huge when I was living in Germany. They were a British band with all the hits in Germany, like "Here's a Heart Crying Out." It

LOBOTOMY

turned out that Dave was now a record executive for my record company, and he held a dinner to meet me. When I got there, I went straight to the bathroom and snorted some British heroin. A couple of lines. Everyone said, "Don't do too much! It's really strong." So, of course I did as much as possible, snort snort snort.

I sat down next to Paul Cook and Dave Dee and I was so happy. I said, "Davy, I really love your . . ." And I threw up in my dinner.

He was very nice about it all. He said, "Oh well, it must be jet lag."

And I said, "Yeah, excuse me, I'm sorry." But inside I was thinking, how can I fuck this up? This is my big chance to meet Dave Dee and everybody is laughing at me. Why do I fuck everything up, always? I was miserable, full of guilt, and thinking, *Do they know, do they know?* Of course they knew.

SOMEHOW, I found a program. I read about it in the back of the *Village Voice*: Drug Program. I walked straight into the Odyssey House on 6th Street and said, "I want to get off drugs."

They didn't like me one bit.

But I wanted justice.

I wanted some kind of personal justice.

I was just getting started. I wanted to live.

YEARS LATER, when I was in rehab, they were asking about the people I knew who had died. And they asked me about Connie. They asked me if I had a chance to mourn her.

Surviving the Ramones

That hit me hard. Mourn somebody? I'm not a cold-blooded person; if anything I'm overly sensitive. But I had never been able to show any grief for Connie. I sat down and wrote about how I wished she could have died.

They buried Connie in Potter's Field. And some girls put their money together for a funeral—then they just went and spent the money on dope.

Alligator Alley

When I got into rap I didn't exactly win any popular-

ity contests. I called myself Dee Dee King, after B.B. King,

to the total dismay of my fellow Ramones. Billboard called

my solo album, *Standing in the Spotlight*, a great party

album and even said that my raps put the Beastie Boys to

shame. *Standing in the Spotlight* included some great

LOBOTOMY

experiments in rap and rock'n'roll, and featured cameos by Chris Stein and Debbie Harry. I loved rap, especially in the early days. But I wasn't trying to shove it down anybody's throats. I didn't have the confidence to leave the band because of a solo career, or anything like that. I just wanted to grow.

Still, the Ramones didn't want change. They thought punk rock fans would hate me for my solo rap record. Which was bullshit.

When I showed up for the video shoot for the Ramones' "I Wanna Live" in a a maroon jumpsuit, gold chains, and a kangol that I'd bought at Doctor Jay's in Flushing, the rest of the band hit the ceiling. If they had had it with me at this point, then fine, I'd sure had it with them. I had a real bad hangover and felt suicidal. It's funny that I was going to do a video for a song called "I Wanna Live." I wanted to die.

Marc Bell came to my rescue. He still saw some worth in me as a songwriter for the band, and was worried about his future. He had bills to pay. That's normal. It was also his turn to keep it together. Marc tried the good-bunny approach.

"Good little bunny," he remarked. "How's my little bunny today? Stop complaining, and don't worry Dee Dee. You're loved."

"I am?" I said, getting all starry-eyed and falling for it.

"Remember, Dee Dee," said Marc, "the good bunny gets the carrot. Carrots are good. Remember, we are bunny men and we need our carrots."

I walked out of the video shoot with him, me trailing slightly behind Marc. He was trying to keep me calm, and then, before I knew what happened, he grabbed my arm and twisted it behind my back. Marc is a big strong guy. There was nothing I could do. He snatched my 007 out of my sock and with his free hand he took the eight-ball that was stashed under my kangol.

The video director had had it with me, though. He wanted to sue me. The whole thing got so complex. I don't really know what I had done that was so serious. I had to sign a paper for everybody to stay out of court. Then we got on a small plane and flew to Atlanta to play a show so they could get live footage for the video. They also had us playing a show in New York at a club called the Ritz, which I couldn't make because I was so nervous.

Marc Bell saved the day, I guess. He had a couple of friends from Brooklyn that he sometimes associated with. They were very much like the types in *The Honeymooners*, the old TV show starring Jackie Gleason. One of the cool things about Marc is the Brooklyn in him. It's his toughness and his sweetness. It makes him seem out of place in somewhere like Florida. But, we were playing a lot of shows down south and heading from Georgia, through Alabama, toward Florida, driving down the highway in our Ramones van with Monte behind the wheel. The usual deal for us. We were all pretty cheerful, and expecting that "I Wanna Live" would be a big hit, and that they were gonna play it on MTV every day—we were already counting the money. We pulled over to a Stuckey's gas station and peanut store, and there was Zippy, a friend of Marc's from Brooklyn. Zippy was gassing up his car. His car seemed pretty comfy, and the Ramones van seemed very stuffy, so we asked Zippy, "Where you going, dude?"

"Florida, my friends, Florida. Miami, Florida, to be exact. Yes, yes, yes, my friends, even Zippy gets a little vacation sometimes."

"Can we come?" Marc and I asked. "We're playing Miami tonight. It would be cool to hang out. Three guys from New York in Florida—pretty hot, dudes! Let's go!"

Monte was pretty pissed off. I think Joey was glad to see us go, so Marc and I got in the car with Zippy and we headed down toward the sun and fun and Miami Beach. All our antennas were up and we were thriving.

The gossip was getting hot after about an hour. Zippy had all kinds of health problems since we had last seen him. I had a million questions to ask him about liver repair and liver damage. We were all wondering about guns, as you could buy them over the counter in Florida. Along the way, people were selling firecrackers and peaches by the road.

It was cool, but soon I began to notice that there were only weeds along the highway. For a long time we seemed to be driving through a swamp. Alligators were peeking at us from the bush, and I saw a snake crawl across the road real fast as we drove by. Zippy tried to run over it, and instead ran the car off the road. We were out of gas anyway, so I don't know if anything could have helped us.

As soon as the car careened off the highway, the weeds all around us caught fire from the heat of the exhaust pipes under the car. The weeds were very dry from the summer heat. The swamp is known as Alligator Alley, hundreds and hundreds of miles of wilderness that runs along one of the highways to Miami. It is not exactly a pleasant place to get stranded. We jumped out of the car and seconds later it burst into flames and started to sink slowly into what seemed like a quicksand pit.

Marc had promised Monte that he would take care of me, and that we would make the show, so he was beside himself. We were all sort of enjoying it, but I was pretty paranoid. The alligators were all flopping and spinning on the highway, where we were all huddled together to escape the flames. I was scared shitless of them, with their beady eyes and their sharp teeth. Stay away, ok? The last thing I wanted was to die in Alligator Alley along the highway in Florida. It was insane. Miles of swamp caught fire and burned completely. Later that night, we saw it on TV at the Miami Holiday Inn. I was worried about the police catching up with us, but nothing ever happened.

We had made it to the show in the back of a pick-up truck which Marc eventually flagged down by waving some hundred-dollar bills at a Good Samaritan. An old pick-up truck stopped and drove us to the theater in Miami. We gave the guy three hundred dollars. The fans were lined up on the street to see the Ramones and they couldn't believe it was Marc and me.

"Are you guys the Ramones?"

"Yeah. Excuse us, we have to get inside to do a sound-check," we said as we darted through the stage door. Zippy

LOBOTOMY

was carrying the pinhead sign which he had somehow saved from the fire in the swamp. It was the same one that the Ramones used to the end. Poor Zippy.

However much I tried to hide my feelings, I knew

I couldn't take it any more. It was explained to me that the

Ramones were my job—I had to do my job. But I felt let

down, like I had to do all the work. I hated it. They expect-

ed me to write one song after another, and then have ten

people never say thank you. All they gave me was attitude.

LOBOTOMY

One of our drummers, Richie Beau, was a good song-
writer. He wrote "Somebody Put Something in My Drink."
Joey is a good songwriter. He wrote "Sheena Is a Punk
Rocker," "Beat on the Brat," "Judy Is a Punk," and "I Don't
Care." Together we wrote "Glad to See You Go"—he put
music to my lyrics. Later he wrote "I Wanna Be Sedated,"
"Rock'n'Roll Radio" and a lot of other great Ramones songs.
The whole band wrote "Pinhead," Tommy too. Later with
songs like "Psycho Therapy," I was trying to get Johnny
Ramone to be less cranky, to get him in a better mood. So I
would try to motivate him to get in on songwriting situations,
and not just give him songs. Johnny Ramone gets a co-writ-
ing credit for "Psycho Therapy" but I wrote that. I could go
on and on.

It was a little absurd. I knew Joey and me were pretty
helpless. We needed a lot of dedicated watching and baby-
sitting. But too much control was in the hands of the music
business people, management, and the record company.
Johnny was making too many musical decisions for a person
who wasn't a songwriter. I wish he had been the one writing
the songs. Nothing would have made me happier. He should
have had the relationship with the management that I had to
put up with. That was like living in hell. When you are on
tour, having the management call you every day at six in the
morning, asking if you have a new song, when you're just trying to get to bed, someone else in the band has been in your
room for four hours on coke telling you he's going to quit
because he's so miserable, and you've got so many bills and
you don't want to write another song—you just hope that

someone else in the band will write, too. It got on my nerves. Johnny just criticized everything. It seemed to be his way of having fun.

It was tough recording the *Brain Drain* album because everyone took their shit out on me. I dreaded being around them. It drove me away—I didn't even end up playing on the album. Everybody in the band had problems; girlfriend problems, money problems, mental problems. It's not easy to be in the same rock'n'roll band with the same people for as long a time as the Ramones were. It just amazed me that people could keep believing in that happy family image of the Ramones. But then, I was amazed when Ricky Nelson died a drug addict. I couldn't believe it. I thought he was such a nice guy, nice songs, he was like an all-American guy. Also, when Del Shannon shot himself, it made me think of why I wanted to shoot myself, too.

Somehow we loved each other though. I was staying in the band because I was so helpless and confused, but also because I was worried about them. How they felt. If they were happy, stuff like that. I worried especially about Joey.

I took a lot of abuse for being a Ramone. Once, I arrived at a New York airport with Monte, and the rest of the Ramones were already waiting. They all looked really uptight. I walked up to Johnny and said, "John, what's goin' on?"

John answered, "I hate him," referring to Joey.

He looked pretty scary, his eyes looked like those of a killer, and he was enraged. Then he scowled at me, and said, "I am not going to Toronto, Dee Dee. I hate him. He used

LOBOTOMY

the name Ramone to play the Ritz." He was referring to a solo gig Joey had played.

"It was a party, John. Joey needs another outlet, it's not . . ."

John cut me off. "No way! No way! It's all or nothing! Fuck everybody. I quit! I don't need this shit!"

"Well, should I go see what Joey thinks?"

"Fuckin' go ahead!" John shot back at me.

So I walked up to Joey, who was glaring at me and John from across the room. He was obviously not going to give an inch.

"Joey, my man. How are you today?" I asked.

"Fuck you, Dee Dee, you're John's friend. I am not going to Toronto today, ok? So fuck all of you."

"Now Joe bro', my man. Remember, sweet lovable all-important one, good bunnies get the carrots. Sweet bunnies with fluffy ears and tails. We are rabbits. Rabbits can't get jobs, Joey. Let's get on the plane. There are places to go and pleasures to enjoy. It's a beautiful day! What are ya' worried about?"

Finally, Johnny Ramone ended up yelling at me in Gary Kurfirst's office one more time. Fuck this, I thought to myself. No more! Why couldn't Monte have crashed the van and gotten us all killed? It seemed like I spent most of my life on the pavement, so it would have been perfect to die on the highway, but that would have been too easy.

If the van had crashed we all probably would have survived, except for Monte. That would have been hilarious. I could just see our sweet Monte going through the windshield. Somehow his head would get chopped off. All our eyes would start sparkling. Johnny Ramone would be thrilled. He would flash us a "how could something this wonderful happen to us" grin, and we would all agree. The air would seem like it had twice as much oxygen, and we would gather around the van and stare at Monte's headless body like a bunch of evil bats. Someone would say, "I've finally seen some justice in my lifetime."

Marky would be dancing around with glee, chuckling "Chicken beak boy! Chicken beak boy!"

Joey would just stand there, twirling a lock of his hair, muttering "Fuck you, Monte . . . Fuck you, Monte . . ."

Johnny Ramone would be pleased as if it were Christmas and there was a Christmas tree with nothing but presents for him under it.

End of the Road

I was learning to appreciate life in the moment, struggling

to learn to be reasonable and have gratitude. Still, no one

would leave me alone. Everybody wanted me to be this or

that, something else, a rock star. And I didn't want to be a

rock star. I wanted to hide, to recover. I wanted to learn

something about music.

LOBOTOMY

I started listening to music again. I hadn't listened to music in thirty damn years. All my records. Day and night. Just saturating myself with music. What everybody wanted out of me was another Ramones album. But I was more interested in my old records.

I'm not a dreamer. I didn't dream my life away, like they thought. I always had a plan; I was always a hard-working person. It was easy for them to ridicule me and ridicule music, when I had to slave away over it.

But I love songs, and I love writing songs. I'm a very visual person, with an investigative nature. And I've been in so many different positions in life, from the lowest to the highest. I've seen it all, and it's all open to me. There's nothing hidden in life to me.

I finally realized that I didn't need to criticize myself so much. I learned to think about my good points. I got very into shao-lin and doing animal forms in the morning. I set myself free.

I believe in God, I have a faith, of protection. I'm not going to will my way through life because I have a protector and He cares about me. He's not going to let me down. He's teaching me.

I learned that I have a good heart, that I don't have to live in fear and hurt people before they hurt me.

And the warfare? There's no time for that for me.

ONE OF the last van rides I took with my "brudders" was on our 1989 US tour, in California. It was one of my many breaking points with them. I was seriously ill at that point. I couldn't stop throwing up. You couldn't tell how skinny I was because I was on Stelazine, Buzzbar, and Trofennial. I was on large doses of these antidepressants to take the edge off being sober. Like Marc and John, I had been sober for a few years by then. Joey was drinking like a fish and causing a lot of trouble, which Marc and John seemed to ignore.

I was convinced that they were trying to force me out of the band. Maybe they sensed that their touring days were numbered. I don't really know why. It seemed to me that they were being unbelievably cruel. I was trying to ignore it, but it hurt. Every time I threw up there would be some sort of mock concern—nobody seemed to realize that being anorexic is so humiliating. How can you talk about that with people who hate you? Anyway, I didn't ask for any favors from them because I knew I wouldn't get any. Even from Monte, who was like a nursemaid to Joey by then, and a slave to the whims of Johnny Ramone.

We traveled all over California on that tour, listening to baseball on the radio all the time. Finally, at one point, I popped a Reba McIntyre cassette into the deck. I wanted to hear the track "Cathy's Clown," but they popped it right out of the deck.

"Forget it, Dee Dee," they said. Well, I guess I was used to it and didn't say anything—they wouldn't listen to my Motorhead tapes either when I first discovered them. Most of the time I would just sit in the back of the van staring out of the window.

By the time we got to San Francisco, we had a day off. I had finally kicked the antidepressants, so I was feeling very

LOBOTOMY

ill. But Monte wouldn't take me to the hospital because Johnny and Joey wanted to go shopping for old movie posters, which they both collect for a hobby.

I was really sick, so I got in a cab and found a clinic and went in for a check-up. The doctor told me that from being anorexic, I had a dead battery. It was suggested to me that I couldn't go on like this, and that I might have as little as three weeks to live.

In a band, on tour, if you're sick, you're sick, but the show must go on. So I finished the tour. The last show I did with them was in Santa Clara, California. Murphy's Law was opening for the Ramones. They were great, but there was some trouble, and Jimmy Gestapo threatened to kick Johnny Ramone's ass. I don't know what the problem was. Then Jimmy said that John would never be safe in New York. I wondered if that meant the rest of the Ramones as well. I was worried.

So, I bailed out. Like Reba sang in "Cathy's Clown," "a man shouldn't crawl . . ." Fuck it, I thought, I can make my life better than this. I want a little more than this crap I get all the time for being Dee Dee Ramone. I felt like I had paid enough dues to the whole damn system and I knew I was man enough to get out of it. After the flight back to New York, I went home to Whitestone, packed a small bag, and left, never to return.

The only thing left to do was to walk out and go back

to my roots. So I moved back to Manhattan and got an

apartment on 10th Street in the East Village. I put my gui-

tar, my records, and a mattress up there.

This was 1989, and everything in the East Village was

still like it used to be. The whole atmospere reeked of

drugs. I was shocked at how bad everyone had ended up—
Stiv Bators, Richard Hell, Johnny Thunders, Cheetah
Chrome. All my friends had no career and were broke, home-
less, or hustling on the street for drugs. You don't get any
sympathy when you're a down-and-out rock star.

Back in Manhattan, I felt kind of edgy. I could hear all the
noises on the street from my apartment window, which had
a nice view of one of the top dope spots. The city looked
weird to me, but I soon got the courage up to scramble down
the stairs and hit the street.

Walking between First and Second Avenues, you have to
walk through a maze of dope dealers and addicts. I scooted
past them to Second and St. Mark's Place, and then walked
up to Third Avenue, where I ran into Johnny Thunders by the
Continental Divide. He looked bad. He was shaking and
obviously needed a fix. We started talking and John asked me
if I wanted to go to where he was staying at a friend's place.

His friend lived at Astor Place, which was nearby. Johnny
went right into the bathroom and shot up some cocaine. His
friend's apartment was pretty nice and I was glad to be there.
I put on a tape of Johnny's new songs and they were really
good. The tape player had a problem, however, and ate up
the tape.

"Shit, Dee Dee," Johnny said to me, "that was the only
copy of those songs! I'll never be able to remember them any
more. Oh, well," and he laughed that crazy sick laugh of his,
which sounded to me like someone's fingernails scratching
down a chalkboard. "Fuck, man, the tape is ruined! I could
have traded it to Billy my dealer for some blow!"

Finally, he got tired of complaining and we decided to walk back over to my apartment on 10th Street. When we got upstairs, he asked me if I had any spoons. Since I wasn't doing dope, I had a bunch of them. He took one and went into the bathroom. Later, I saw the spoon. It was bent over and had been burned on the bottom of it to cook up some dope. A little piece of cotton, pink with blood, was still in the center of the spoon. I picked it up and threw it into the trash can by the toilet. What a bunch of loser friends I have, I thought to myself. It seemed to me that this Lower East Side lowlife stuff had been following me around for ever.

After I left the Ramones, I didn't talk to the other guys. I didn't see anyone. As soon as the good times and the money were gone, it was just me again. No one wanted to know. The typical show business type of thing.

I know the Ramones management didn't know what to do with me. When I went to see Gary Kurfirst, he didn't have anything positive to say about me getting a new band together. Everyone at Sire Records was unapproachable. The only thing Gary could think of was that the Ramones might need some more songs, so he sent me to see Andrea Starr, who worked for the Ramones management at Overland. Andrea seemed to be on my side. She and I had always gotten along in the past. Andrea had also tried to help me with my *Dee Dee King* album, but it was in vain. My *Dee Dee King* rap album was me trying to write in an imaginary way, not auto-biographically—giving myself an assignment. I can write what I want to but I don't want to play the music business game. That's me. Dee Dee. But I could tell that Andrea did-

LOBOTOMY

n't know what to do with me either. I guess everyone could tell that I was about to go through another bad period in my life, and they had their own troubles.

I was at the bottom of everyone's list.

Survivor

PART FIVE

Paris

The Ramones were behind me. Dee Dee King was

behind me. Dope was behind me. I was ready for a new life.

Andrea was friends with Stiv Bators, who had recently

left The Lords of the New Church. She suggested that I get

out of New York for a while, and hook up with Stiv and try

to start up a band in Paris. It was supposed to be with Chris

LOBOTOMY

from the Godfathers on guitar, Vom from Dr. and The Medics on drums, and me on bass. I told Andrea and she said to discuss it with Stiv, which I did. I called Stiv in Paris and told him I'd come, but not if Thunders was there. I told him about what had happened the last time I was with Thunders, and Stiv agreed with me. So I flew over to Paris to stay with Stiv and his girlfriend Carol. It was ok, but a little creepy for some reason. It was always cold, and if I got a chill, Stiv would say, "Oh, that's just 'cause the devil is here with us."

Thunders was there too—he was sad, angry, and mad, all at once. They also had a big black cat called Satan, which used the kitchen sink to go to the bathroom. Christ Almighty! And Thunders was doing everything possible to get me to do dope.

It's too bad. Thunders, Stiv, and I could have had quite a band. We did try to go to one rehearsal together, though, but we just sat around and couldn't get it together. We each had an acoustic guitar, and were playing 1950's Dion and the Belmonts material. Nothing was really happening, though. Stiv was very broken down from his days in London and he told me that his liver was only 80 percent functioning.

Meanwhile, Carol was trying to run the show, pointing out everything we were doing wrong. "Put down that twelve-string, Stiv," she'd say to him. "No one wants to hear any silly love songs from you." Carol does have good taste in music.

I could also tell that Stiv, John, and I were not going to get anywhere as a "three guys from New York act." But I knew that I needed to do something, so I woke Stiv up and marched him upstairs, where I had a live mic and my stacks set up, along with a wah-wah pedal and a distortion unit. I had my bass and I was ready.

"Stiv, I want you to shout *shit!* and *fuck!* and *piss!* into the mic as I am going at it, ok?"

"Ok, Doug," Stiv replied. He had a happy/sad/I-am-confused face on, but lord knows what he was really thinking. I saw that same look on Brian James's face a year or two later at the Gold, in Portobello in London. In fact Stiv was staring at a mouse that had been caught in one of their traps—there were so many mice and rats in the apartment that Carol had to put out traps because Satan couldn't catch all of them. The mouse was not quite dead, and was still twitching. Stiv caught its eye before it died, and said in a thick German accent, "All good cretins go to heaven!"

I couldn't believe it, so I started playing my bass like a maniac possessed by some evil spirit. But I couldn't get Stiv to react. He couldn't stand up for too long any more, and he fainted. He tried to shout something once or twice, I'll give him that. But no cigar. Being in the Lords of the New Church with Brian James had fucked him up too much. I picked him up and carried him downstairs to his bed.

I didn't know that Carol was in the bed also, but she was. She lifted up the covers and peered at me. Her hair was disheveled and her eyes were glowing like two yellow coals. Under the covers in the darkened room, she looked somehow like a snake. Carol was only half awake, but I had disturbed her and I knew she could be a hassle, so I decided to try to charm her.

"Oh, Carol, baby. Sweet darling, how are you? I was just

LOBOTOMY

finding some dope for you and Stiv, but I decided to bring Stiv to you first. Now I will run upstairs and fetch some dope. Then I will be right back. Carol, you would like some dope if I have some, wouldn't you? Don't worry, I have some. I'm going to fetch it now. Trust me."

"Oh, Dee Dee!" Carol shrieked with delight. "This sounds quite lovely!"

It was one of the first times I had ever seen her come so to life. When she smiled, I noticed something however—two fangs appeared to be coming out of her mouth! I had never noticed them before, and they reminded me that I had better get going while the going was good. I had been bullshitting Carol, though, and now I was in a trap because of my own stupidity. I had to make good and get the dope. Everybody was waiting. The whole household was disrupted and they were blaming me.

So, I got the dope and went back to the apartment. Then we all played a game of Vietnamese Roulette, which is the same as Russian Roulette, except that the desensitization is done with opium instead of with lead. I loaded the poisoned hypodermic and fired it. It bit deep and filled me with intense hatred.

One of the last things that happened in Paris which really pissed me off was another bad scene between me and Johnny Thunders. A *bad* one. I was convinced he had been stealing things from me ever since I had arrived, but I couldn't prove it. Then I caught him red-handed. My coat had gone missing and I found it in his suitcase. I don't care if he was Johnny Thunders or whoever. I was fed up with being so nice. I just lost it with all of them and made a big scene.

The next day I took a cab to the airport and bought a ticket back to New York. I had tried my hardest with Stiv while I was in Paris. I just couldn't get a break, though. I had put the emphasis on trying to write songs with him, or getting a band together with him and Thunders, but nothing worked. I couldn't penetrate the barrier that Stiv and Thunders had wrapped around themselves. It was like that in the Ramones. I couldn't penetrate the barrier around them either. Eventually the Ramones became a clique, and I felt excluded from it.

It was ridiculous, trying to please people who can't be pleased. I ended up friendless anyway. I knew that all my so-called friends back in New York would take Thunders' or Stiv's side over what had happened in Paris. In addition, no one understood why I left the Ramones, and it wasn't a very popular decision. It was not going to be a very good time in life.

After I left Paris, Stiv politely tried to steal my song "Poison Heart." I had a tape of it in my suitcase. When I got back to New York, it wasn't there. Stiv went to England and recorded a demo of it. It would be too painful now for me to hear the actual demo—after all, I am the only survivor of the three of us. Although at the time no one thought I would outlive Johnny or Stiv. As for Stiv, I always thought that behind his Joey Ramone shades and hairstyle, there was a punk rock singer, so I forgive him. RIP, Stiv.

New York seemed very cold when I got back.

Things had changed. If I wanted to break my isolation I

was going to invite trouble. The Ramones had sort of been

my family—now there was nothing. It was also a setup for

disaster living on 10th Street again. Everybody in the

LOBOTOMY

neighborhood dealt dope—one of my old cocaine dealers even lived in the same building as me.

I never realized life could be so grim. Finally, when I hit the street I was lonely and tired of having conversations with myself. I started thinking that I could justify anything, so I started getting high again. All the dealers were more than happy to have a big spender around. They gave me attention and made me feel like I was very special. When I was stoned, I would sit on the stoop with them and spin fantastic tales about all my adventures.

During September, when I went to the guitar shop on the Lower East Side, I noticed people selling dope in the area, so I went there to cop some. It was on 13th Street and Avenue C. There was an abandoned building on the corner where they sold heroin. The brand name for it was "Bulldog." The dope had different brand names and if you were going to cop, you said you were going over to the Bulldog. It was more organized than in the early days of punk rock in New York City.

I started trying to re-live the old days. The old routine. Hitting the sidewalk around 12 o'clock to go cop. Then, on the way home, I would stop at the deli on 10th and First to get some coffee and some cigarettes. I'd try to avoid the street crazies and panhandlers, and as soon as I'd walk out the door of the deli, I would scurry down the sidewalk and up the stairs to my apartment. In my bathroom I'd shoot up like Thunders did when I had him over. The bathroom was a good place to get high and forget where you were. You could observe reality down below on the street if you wanted to.

Surviving the Ramones

This is sort of traditional New York behavior—staring out the window in a daze. I loved to do it.

It would always be real noisy and confusing down there. A madhouse of activity all day and all night—people hustling dope on the street. The customers want it, but it's cold. The freezing winter cold makes the chill in a junkie's bones even worse. No one's in the mood for any bullshit. In the city, it's animal eat animal. Man is a dangerous predator. You have to be on the ball. You risk going into debt to your supplier if something goes wrong. You risk going to jail.

Once, when I was looking out the window, I noticed four people who sold dope in the area. You could sense trouble coming. One of the guys down there was my old coke dealer, he was on the lookout for his girl so he didn't see the two enforcers who were about to come down on him. They were blending in with the crowd of street crazies and paranoid customers. It all happened so fast—one of the enforcers had a golf club and the other had a heavy walking stick. They were there to collect money owed to the supplier. They told the girl to hand it over, and started roughing up her man. The dealer's two friends who were across the street ran to help, and then a car, which was parked nearby, pulled away from the curb and stopped right in front of the action. The person on the passenger side of the car stuck a Marlin .22 automatic carbine out of the window. It had a banana clip in it, and he started firing it. At the sound of the shots going off, the whole block scattered. It was like a scene from a movie, but it wasn't. It was real.

The cop cars were there in a minute. I saw them grab the girl. She was in shock and just standing there. The police cuffed her and threw her in the van. The paramedics picked up her boyfriend who had been shot. They lost their dope, their money, and their freedom.

I kept thinking, "Is this any way to live?" Is the system giving us any choice? It's so stupid. Society is burning itself out. American cities are hopeless and it doesn't look like it will ever level off. It makes me wonder how minority groups can survive, because it's even harder when you're hated all your life—no one will give you a break. You're judged guilty before they can prove you did the crime. You live in a war zone and have to fight constantly to survive.

When you're really down, you sense that someone is doing their best to keep the oppressed people oppressed. Drugs keep flowing into poor neighborhoods. It's the easiest thing for a government to do, because they see these people as a problem. They see them as a burden, not as human beings. Even though I was self-supporting, there were people claiming that I was a burden, so they came down on me. I was caught up in the big mess like everyone else—publicly and socially I was an outcast. Who the fuck would care if 10th Street in New York City burned down? We'd just stand there, watch it burn, and breathe in the smoke. Everybody could get one last high for free. What kind of a deal is that?

I only lasted a few months copping dope again in the East Village. I was thirty-eight years old and caught a dope habit again and I couldn't handle it. For the first time in my life I had lost my freedom. I had to go on the methadone program for real. I became doomed to being a lifer in the liquid concentration camp.

Surviving the Ramones

Realistically I don't think anything else could have happened to me at that point. Too much had gone wrong. I had made too many changes without any support system. Instead, there were people really going for me, trying to take me down. Then I got the news that Stiv Bators had been in an accident and gotten killed in Paris. He was hit by a taxi. At about the same time, my best friend, Phil Smith, a pot dealer in New York, died of AIDS. Then, I found out my girlfriend was a whore. Finally, I got on the subway one day at Astor Place and took the Lexington Avenue local uptown to the celebrity methadone clinic on 69th Street and First Avenue.

I hated my life. I sort of wished I was dead. Being a methadone patient was like the end of the line. I had no choice. I had no Blue Cross insurance, so I couldn't get into a rehab. I tried to go to an AA meeting and an NA meeting, but they just put me in a worse mood. Especially the Artists' and Musicians' Meeting at St. Mark's Place. There was just no way I was going to go cold turkey and stay off dope and live in the East Village. There were a million other reasons too, so the methadone progam was the best I could do to manage my life as a junkie at that point. Methadone didn't exactly put me in a good mood. When I left the clinic and rode the subway back downtown I always felt worse. That's why I started referring to the program as the liquid concentration camp.

In my weak state of mind, I was totally defenseless. On the surface, it might seem hard to believe that people would go out of their way to hurt me. I mean, why bother? Why? Because of my money. What could be more logical than for my enemies to run me around in circles until I was so dizzy that I didn't know what I was doing any more. The only way I could fix the pain was the only way I ever knew how—to run to the cooker. Drugs are the killer's dream. It's not fair, but that's how it is.

It was after I had been arrested twice for possession of pot that things took a turn for the worse. The first time I was defending my girlfriend on the subway. The second time I was walking by this club in New York called The Bottom Line. All of a sudden, the cops swarmed on me. They cuffed me and threw me into the police van. They picked up everyone who looked a little weird—it was a sweep. When the police van was nice and stuffed, they drove it to Washington Square Park and parked it by the fountain. The press had been notified ahead of time. That's why they made such a big deal out of it: so it would appear that the city was winning the war against drugs.

They made the news. They had caught a hardened criminal.

Me.

Dee Dee Ramone.

They photographed me all the way to the precinct, and then threw me in jail. I was real fucking mad by then. I protested everything, which delighted them even more. The next day, my picture was on the front page of the New York *Post*. Somehow that picture makes me laugh today. I looked like a madman, but then again, I was tattooed, ripped, and unsmiling. I was real damn angry! I'm not a judge, and I do not think that weed should be illegal, but if I did have to be punished, what was the big deal, considering how harmless

Surviving the Ramones

my crime was anyway? Lisa Robinson, the rock columnist of the New York *Post*, who never had a good word for me ever, wrote a piece about me supposedly passing out with a needle in my arm in the bathroom of a club on Bleeker Street in the West Village.

Then the Ramones' management turned on me. They took advantage of my bad luck streak, and strung me along to get material for a new Ramones' album. I sold the publishing rights to "Poison Heart," "Main Man," and "Strength to Endure" for a few thousand dollars so I could hire a lawyer to get out of jail. I don't know why no one in New York, or none of the Ramones, couldn't have loaned me a few thousand dollars, instead of forcing me to go through all the paranoia, confusion, and extra pain of a maneuver like that. And to top it off, these songs ended up on a new Ramones album called *Mondo Bizarro*.

It seemed that the Ramones couldn't live without me, but at the same time they treated me like an enemy. I considered it vain and stupid on their part, but it was probably the only way they could save face. To build up the Ramones, they had to keep running me down. In interviews they were obviously trying to play down my role as a writer—"Dee Dee co-wrote it." *No*, I wrote it with all my heart and soul. "Poison Heart" was *my* song about *my* life.

At the same time, a hate campaign started against me. There were all sorts of rumors. That I was going crazy. That I was shooting pistols off on the street. That I stole a loaf of bread from the supermarket. That I was killing cats in my apartment. Everyone seemed to have their own idea about

LOBOTOMY

what I was doing. Nobody bothered to find out the truth from me—the only person I was having conversations with at this point was myself. I am pretty much antisocial anyway. Everyone else I knew was dead, or some kind of rock and roll casualty. I was lonely. The depression drove me straight back to drugs.

I felt like Public Enemy Number One—so I tried staying out of the East Village for a while. It was too hot for me on 10th Street, so I got a little apartment on 23rd and Lexington and tried to hide out. They had a methadone clinic in the neighborhood. The methadone patients were so stoned that they would stand on the street and sway in the wind. They never completely tipped over—somehow they would wake up for a moment and sway back the other way. They were real fucked up.

My friend, Mark Brady, was trying to lift me above this B-movie mentality. He was a good friend and a good influence on me at the time. I met him through Rachel Amado, who had the lead role in a movie which Mark was making, called *What About Me?* which also starred Johnny Thunders, Richard Hell, Nick Zed, and Jerry Nolan. I wish Mark still had my phone number, and would give me a call.

Mark was trying to motivate me, so he gave me a small part in the movie. After we finished my scene, we called it a wrap and went over to Rachel's apartment to relax and smoke some weed. When we got there the phone rang. It was Stevie, the guitar player in Johnny Thunders' band.

"Rachel," he said, "John died. He's dead."

I was stunned. So was Rachel. Six months earlier Stiv

Surviving the Ramones

Bators had died. My friend Phil Smith had just died. Life seemed so fragile. All the memories started flashing before me. They told me that Johnny had gotten mixed up with some bastards down in New Orleans, who had ripped him off for his methadone supply. They had given him LSD, and then murdered him. He had gotten a pretty large supply of methadone in England, so he could travel and stay away from those type of creeps—the drug dealers, Thunders imitators, and losers like that. Life seemed pretty cheap at that moment. I got up and left. I didn't care if I died next.

No matter how many differences Johnny and I had, I was miserable when I found out that he was dead. Everybody seemed to be fighting a drug problem. There was all this finger-pointing going on, that I would be next. It really pissed me off, and I made a vow that I would not die because of drugs, just to spite my enemies.

But I was still out of control. I was trying my hardest, but the reality was that the methadone wasn't blocking my craving for street drugs. I was still hell-bent on self-destruction. Mark Brady was worried that I would go on a binge when Thunders died. He was right. I shot up quarter-grams of cocaine for a couple of days. Then I went over to the Continental Divide for a tribute concert for John. The warm-up band was a '70s Dolls–type of band, with a guitarist who was a Thunders imitator. They were playing "Chinese Rocks" as I went in. I turned pale and left immediately. It was too much for me. Instead, I went down to the Bowery and got drunk. The next day I shot up some dope. I just didn't give a damn any more.

233

LOBOTOMY

I hated my life. I was living in a flophouse on 23rd Street and taking the subway to the methadone clinic every day. In the morning I would get the *Post*. In the afternoon I would go cop some pot. I needed to get myself into a rehab program, but I didn't have the money. It was the holiday season and Christmas was the worst. One of my neighbors didn't like the fact that when I stepped out of my room I would slam the door. I tried to reason with him. My lawyer had explained to me that if I was arrested a third time, I would have to go upstate to prison. I already had two arrests behind me—one of which was for felony assault. I ended up kicking my neighbor's ass in the hallway anyway. Then I bade him a Merry Christmas and went to the Scrap Bar to celebrate, as I had nothing else to do.

I ran into Lemmy from Motorhead. He took one look at me and he told me I looked terrible. I knew that. He didn't look so great himself, but I was always glad to see him. I was hoping that he had some drugs. He didn't, but he gave me a small loan, a beer and some free advice—"Get out of New York, Dee Dee. Go to Los Angeles."

So I went home and decided to go to England. Carol Bators gave me the information on how to switch programs, as she had done it many times. I guess that Carol knew every trick in the book. I got it together the best that I could. I scammed four bottles of methadone to take with me on the plane. Then I got in a cab and took myself to the airport. I bought a ticket, got in a plane, and flew to London. I know that the only reason I am still alive is because I left New York.

Westbourne Park

Everywhere I went, I was in exile. The customs officials at Gatwick didn't want to let me into England even though all the drugs I had on me were given to me legally by a doctor. I have always felt the wrath of discrimination every time I cross a border. As for the treatment

LOBOTOMY

I have gotten at places like Gatwick Airport Customs, all I can say is that it was very demoralizing.

Somehow, I made it through all that, found a taxi and got to Earl's Court, where my hotel was. I was worried about how I'd get to my program because it was outside of London, in Hayes, Kent. I called Ira, my friend and business manager in New York, to ask him what to do. I was becoming overwhelmed, and when he suggested I take the train, I panicked. So I took another cab. English cab drivers are the worst, and they charge a lot—about the same as a fix. I wanted to get off drugs, so I just put up with it. I was very weak, and tried not to make small talk with the smiling freak who was driving me. He let me out in front of an old, haunted-looking house, where the drug program was located. I rang the bell and waited by the door until the nurse let me in. I was taken up a creaky, winding staircase to see my doctor. He was a nice guy, but kinda nutty. He asked me to explain my demons, but I wouldn't say anything. He was used to working with dishonest addicts and remained pretty cheerful. I got a three-week scrip for methadone. We said good-bye and I promised to be good. The receptionist called me a cab. The fare was a third of the previous fare, which made me very happy. I took the cab to the Flora Hotel in Earl's Court, my new home for the time being.

The Flora was right around the corner from the Boots drugstore. I would go there every day, pick up a quart bottle of methadone and drink it, hidden in a Boots bag, in one of those red, London-style phone booths. That was breakfast. All I could think of was how low I had fallen. Doing drugs on the street again, and in a phone booth! Oh well, no one seemed to care what I was doing anyway.

The only person who talked to me, and seemed to care how I was doing, was Mr. Jefferies. I met him at the prescription counter at Boots. He was an old junkie and had to walk to Boots every day on two crutches because he was a cripple. He was a real survivor, and a success, for his type. He had been on dope for thirty years and had gotten his first scrip at sixteen. He, too, had a room in one of the hotels around Earl's Court. He invited me to come over and hang out. He said that if I was ever stranded, I could crash on his floor. No one else had even talked to me, and here this guy was opening his door to me. I guess he needed a friend. I had learned a long time ago not to make friends, so I didn't really say that much to him. He had been around, and was the same type as me—a street rat. He asked me at once why I wasn't using the needle. That I could get anything at the program at this point. I told him that I wanted to quit.

"Why?" he asked.

"You know why," I replied.

That was about it. Two social deviants struggling in the spider's web and pretty hopelessly trapped. I planned it that if I was still in England at Christmas I would go over to his room to celebrate.

Then, I met an Irish fellow in a pub who told me about a room available in Westbourne Park. He said it was a good deal, and took me to meet a German woman who wanted to rent it. When he showed up later to meet me by the tube station, he was fucked up on Ecstasy—a drug I later decided

LOBOTOMY

that they should call "agony." It didn't matter, I was feeling better. I liked Westbourne Park. It was a nice working-class area, and I liked the canal and the bridge. It didn't look like any place in New York. Perhaps the closest thing would have been Forest Hills in Queens. When we went over to the flat to meet the landlady, she said I could take the room. It was nothing special, and perhaps I would have been better off staying in Earl's Court. At least no one at the Flora was sleazy. But I had already made up my mind and I took the room. I didn't have to give her a deposit because she was so happy to have someone take the place off her hands. It was pretty crummy, but the best I could do. I was happy to have a roof over my head, and tried to make small talk with her. I guess she liked me, and we decided to go for a walk in the Portobello Road area, where all the flea-market stalls are. On Saturdays this area would be buzzing and now I could walk to Kensington Market to look at clothes. I felt cool, like I was really living in London now.

I liked my new neighborhood a lot. There was a pub that we walked past called the Portobello Gold. It was described to me as "The Rockers' Graveyard," and I was told that it would be a good place for me to hang out and that you could cop dope in the area.

All the babes in London looked very flash, like they never do anywhere else. I was getting restless. One night, I cracked and took the tube to the Marquee to see the Phantom Chords. The Marquee Club was filled with vampire types, and with my colorless blood, plum hair, and pale complexion, I fit right in. I started prowling around, and soon I spotted what would have been a perfect victim for me maybe ten years ago or so. She was all dolled up in a patent leather mini and spiked heels and she had that blond baby-doll hair. She looked like pure sex, but for once I turned down the chance for some excitement because I knew I couldn't take it. We were both too tired, anyway. She was worn out by her lifestyle. And life had just about gotten the best of me by then. We did hang out a bit, and the next day we went to see a movie, and went to Häagen Däaz for ice cream. As we were strolling around Piccadilly Circus, we passed a hotel, and the babe made some comment like, "Oh, there's the late-night bistro where I go for a coffee when I'm in between jobs."

Well, the usual, right? I'd had enough of that in New York. I looked at that gorgeous creature, and though it was tough, I just said to her, "Oh, isn't that quite jolly," and scampered off towards the tube and just went home alone. I thought about calling her, but never did. I guess that's the price of recovery. You have to start trying to solve your problems instead of creating new ones. The officials at Gatwick had given me a chance to correct my mistakes. I felt as if they were rooting for me to win. I took the chance and did things right for a change.

I wasn't panicking about the thought of death, but something in me was demanding that it was my turn to live. I started defrosting the blood in me. I was gazing over the barbed wire and dreaming about getting out of the liquid concentration camp. It was pretty overwhelming, but I knew I had to change completely. I really felt alone in England, but that was what I needed.

LOBOTOMY

Once, near the Canal Street Bridge, I noticed a group of skinheads. They looked great, dressed in their Doc Marten boots and lightweight army trenches. They were all amped up and ready to swarm in on a possible victim. I was seeing all this as I was walking along, and noticed how gleeful they became when they spotted a "vic." He looked like an unshaven drunk, and the skins didn't like him. One of them walked up to him, and shouted "Good Morning!" into his ear. The next thing the skin did was snatch the guy's cap from his head. I guess they were going to fuck with him, but he had a bald head. The skin gave him a wooden look and let him go. As I was watching this, I thought that maybe I should shave my head too. This is England, right? And this is a grim society which I live in. I am going to have to live by a few rules here, just as I did when I was in the Ramones. This society has no use for weakness. Only the strong survive, and the strong prey on the weak. This is an outlaw society. When you have "Made in England" tattooed on your skull, you live by rules that you learn, by having to fight your way through life, and it doesn't give you much choice.I was trying hard to see something positive in the routine of daily life. I would buy *The Sun* and *The Mirror* at the tube station for the horoscopes, before walking down the Portobello Road to Notting Hill Gate. I would stroll around Kensington Market, and then I'd start back home. The Westbourne Park tube station is a center of low-life activity in the area, and there was always some pitiful sight that would sadden me a little more before I dragged myself home. A week or so before I left London, I was buying the papers there and I saw a beat-up blonde with a child, standing by the payphone at the station. She looked so out of it, so out of place. She was crying, and her big tears were raining down on her baby's face. I guess she'd had a fight with her old man. She probably had had to run for her life. She took her child with her, and now they had nowhere to go.

I walked past them and started on my way home again. As I was crossing over the Canal Street bridge, I noticed a man whom I could sense was the guy she'd had the fight with. I would describe him as a "Disco-Dan" type. He looked like he was trapped forever in re-runs of *Saturday Night Fever*. He was a mess, and with his cheap, lopsided wig on his head, he was embarrassing to look at. He was throwing his life away, and it looked pathetic. He was dead drunk and looked like he had always been that way. I felt like putting him out of his misery and pushing him off the curb and into the traffic. I knew that I was losing it.

It reminded me of something I had once read. An old drunken man walking down 23rd Street pointed it out to me. It was written on the doorframe of the Chelsea Hotel. I had never noticed it before. It read, "The man who says he hates you, hates the human race." That hit home. How could I go through life with so much hostility in me? I had to cut it out. No matter what had happened to me, I had to start surrendering in order to win. If everyone was my enemy, then I had to try and forget it for a while. I had to stop hating everybody. I had to stop hating myself.

I couldn't keep re-living my past and going through the whole routine over and over. I needed a chance to pull myself

LOBOTOMY

together. Seventeen years of touring with the Ramones hadn't been easy. When I was with them, we toured the world by rules that were decided for me—I had no part in making them. I was only allowed to learn them, live by them, and not question them. I had to learn how to just go blank and not think about it.

The Ramones became grim creatures on automatic. When Johnny Ramone would shout a command, we would listen. We would head to the theater for some fun. Whoever made the biggest fuss won. If you didn't win, there was always another game the next day. We were hardened pros. All we needed was a demon drum beat to rip to. When the smoke started fizzling and the speakers were about to blow, we would just stop dead on the beat.

The crackle on stage would get Johnny Ramone to freak out. He would get dangerous, yelling and glaring at everyone. He had nothing but pure hate in his eyes. He hated everyone, especially Joey and me. We loved it. It was fun to watch him go off. There are certain types who can really yell in an extremely hostile manner. I certainly can, my mother can, but John was fantastic at it. He could really make a sour face. In return I have pulled knives on him, yelled the f-word at him, and told him that I hated his guts.

Why we didn't stick together, I don't know. It's hard to get anywhere in life, and when we did, we just threw it all away. I just stood there on the stage, in the midst of all the insanity, and sulked. I knew that sooner or later a maniac lingering on the floor would slither up to me and say, "Hey, man, wanna party?"

Surviving the Ramones

"What the fuck do you think, knucklehead? Dee Dee Ramone is my name. Drugs, booze, and broads are my game. I am down with cocaine, beer, weed, wine, and girls in miniskirts. Also dope, Valium, and Quaaludes."

I knew that Johnny Ramone would be listening. *I don't care*, I thought. Is this a rock band or the fucking army?

In London I couldn't keep going to Boots every day any more. I got tired of the embarrassment of taking the garbage out when the only thing in it was empty methadone bottles, so I used to stack them up in the medicine cabinet. I also had a few full 90 milligram bottles sitting on the shelf in my kitchen cabinet. I had started taking it home and drinking it there.

It dawned on me that the only way forward was to slowly detox myself. I tried to be logical about what I was doing, but, looking back, it was probably pretty stupid to keep the methadone in my flat, but I felt insecure. Every methadone addict worries and worries . . . about earthquakes, or if there is going to be another world war and the hospitals and drug-stores will close. So I kept it around. I wasn't tempted to drink a large dose and get loaded. Instead, I was getting very excited, sort of like I was outracing the devil. The less methadone I had in my system, the more chance I knew I had, and I wanted to make it.

I started drinking three cups a day, which is what the bottle I brought home held. I kept a little chart on the wall, I was determined to get off the methadone, milligram by milligram. Soon I had a bunch of ugly, brown bottles, filled with green poison, sitting in my room.

LOBOTOMY

Sooner or later I knew I was going to have to go home, so finally, I called the accounting service that Ira had found for me to help me through my stay in London. I told them I needed to get home, so they sent a limo to pick me up, enough money to live on, and a Clipper-Class ticket back to New York on Virgin Atlantic Airlines. I was a wreck, but I flew back to New York in style. There was even a limo waiting for me at the airport to take me back to the Chelsea Hotel, where I would be staying.

Before I left London I threw all that green liquid gook down the drain. I didn't want it to get into anyone else's hands. As far as I was concerned, my name was on the bottle, and in anyone else's hands it was illegal. I owed England something for letting me into the country, and this was my way of showing my gratitude.

It was August 28, 1992, when I flew from London back

home to New York. I was trying to hide it, but I was crying.

I think I was crying because I realized I was almost forty

years old and had no home—nowhere to go.

Cold Turkey at the Chelsea

Dee Dee at the Chelsea Hotel *Keith Green*

Surviving the Ramones

All was quiet on the Eastern front. Our East Coast fort was quiet. There was an ice-cool breeze over the city. Sea gulls were gliding closer to the bay. There were new feelings in me.

New York in September has always excited me. It's when you can cruise the sidewalks faster. It's when the summer heat doesn't drag you down. I get fall fever, but I am not sure what I am looking for.

After the plane landed at JFK, I hailed a cab to 23rd Street in Manhattan and checked myself into the Chelsea Hotel. I was lucky I had that. I knew I was going to have to suffer, but I had planned this. I knew what I was in for. To go cold turkey off the methadone. A fight for my life.

I refused all offers of dope from the friends that I used to know that still lived in the hotel. I locked myself up in my room and shut myself off from the whole world. I am stubborn, and was determined to make it through the withdrawal. I plugged up the cracks in the bathroom window and ran the hot water in the shower to steam the methadone out of me. Methadone doesn't lock in your blood, it locks in the marrow of your bones. It's difficult to kick. It's got to leak very slowly out of you. I did everything to help this process along. I shaved my head and clipped my nails to make it come out faster. I made myself eat, and heated up soup on a hot plate. There was no one to take care of me. I kept thinking I really should be dead, but somehow I made it.

Finally, when I thought I could manage it, I decided to face New York again, and hopped into a cab to try and get

LOBOTOMY

some money from my publishers. If innocence is an illusion, then I don't believe it, because there is so much beauty in New York.

I hailed a cab at 57th and Broadway. The driver was a Puerto Rican girl, and she seemed cool. Latin girls always are. They seem to have a more realistic sense of urban survival than the type I used to end up with. She had her hair pulled back, a dark sweatshirt on and regular blue jeans. I got into the cab and politely asked her to take me to the Chelsea Hotel. We smiled at each other, and I felt relieved and glad that I didn't have a nut for a driver. I also felt something else, I'm not sure what. It was a new feeling. It was as if her pride was a turn-on—she was setting a standard for herself.

Les, one of the owners of Chelsea Guitars, the guitar store next door to the hotel, told me that Jerry Nolan was looking for me, and that Jerry was doing ok. Jerry, Les said, had written a story about his life for the *Village Voice*. I wanted to see the story, but I wasn't ready to see Jerry. Everybody told me that he was off drugs and doing real well, but I was worried. Les told me that Jerry got five thousand dollars for the article in the *Village Voice*. If he really has that much money now, I thought to myself, he won't be able to resist. It's too much temptation.

By the time Christmas came around I was crashing on the floor of Mark Brady's loft on 14th Street. We had no heat or hot water. I was very weak. Finally I went to the Astor Place Diner with Mark and another friend of ours to have Christmas dinner. Mine was a cheeseburger, and it looked mighty good. As we were eating, I saw Chrissy, my girlfriend at the time, stroll by the window with three tricks. She could almost have been the reincarnation of Connie. They looked so incredibly alike. Oddly, this was the same neighborhood where Connie had died.

When I was in England I remember reading something in *The Mirror* or *The Sun* that helped me. It was a story about a famous cricket player. He and his wife had broken up, then some reporters found out that his wife was on the game. What the reporters then did was to hire the girl for a photo session. It wasn't pretty. They splashed the story all over the front pages of the papers as well, and in detail. And then they went to interview him to get his reaction to all of this. I thought this would be too much for any man. They hounded him, and even interrupted him in the middle of a cricket match. His reaction was, "Excuse me, I have a game of cricket to play."

I thought this was a brilliant move and I copied it.

"Is that Chrissy?" I asked Mark and his friend.

"Yes, Dee Dee," they told me. "It's her."

They were upset. So was I.

"What do you think?" they asked me.

"Oh, I don't know," I said. "I have a cheeseburger to finish."

Even though I felt sorry for myself and Chrissy, there was nothing I could do about it. I had tried that before. It just ended up bringing me to my knees. Then I would get high. I was lonely, but I was better off without her—Chrissy wasn't worth it. I had to escape drugs, prostitution, and violence. But it hurt. I loved Chrissy too.

LOBOTOMY

On Christmas Day, I sneaked into my old room in the building where I used to live before I left New York, on 23rd and Lexington. This was a real seedy apartment building, which used to be the George Washington Hotel. By chance, one of my old girlfriends came by to see if I was there. She had a shopping bag with her, and I thought that she might have brought me a Christmas present, but she hadn't. She had just come over to add some more hell to my life. She started a fight, and then informed me that she was going to work over at the Executive Spa, a whorehouse on 23rd Street. Believe me, I didn't want a free sample. But I didn't get worked up and shoot dope over it. She was on the game—some things don't change. But I was changing, in my own way. I followed the "You make your own luck" rule.

What helped was that New York had become a big void for me. I didn't fit in. I couldn't relate. Walking around New York already felt like walking around a cemetery for me. Everyone I knew before had pretty much wasted their lives or were dead.

Then Jerry Nolan died. I cried over that. He was some kind of friend. I cared about him, and I looked up to him when I started playing. He had that cool, spiked-blond hair-cut. He was a star, at least in Manhattan, to Dolls' and Heartbreakers' fans like me. I couldn't go to the funeral. I just stood there in a daze after hearing the bad news from Mark Brady. Mark went to the funeral alone.

Mark didn't say much about the funeral when he got home. He was devastated. Jerry had also been a close friend to Mark, and Mark had tried to help him. Now it was too late. We both sank into a valley of pain that was becoming all too familiar. I could hardly breathe. I just ended up walking down one of the cold halls in our squat until I found a dark corner. Another person in my life had just become a memory. Pretty grim. What a business.

The Blues

For fourteen months after returning from England I had

been trying to re-live my lower East Side past. I went to

England to grow up—I had come very close to being a

street junkie or worse. The creepy stuff that I saw along the

way will always be in my memory. Some good came out of

the sad things that happened. I don't think I would be doing

LOBOTOMY

anything if I hadn't seen what happened to Johnny Thunders. After he died, I knew I had to fight. The New York Dolls were a symbol of the old school of New York "rock" and I felt that with his passing, something else died too.

If all this sounds confusing, then how do you think I felt?

I felt doomed. As an ex-Ramone, I was already too damaged by my past to expect anything else.

Now I am just trying to get over my amazement that I made it through all that, and I am still alive. My life is getting better. I've been through a lot.

If you believe the old saying that you have to live the blues to play the blues, then I guess I am pretty damned experienced. Someone once told me that good thing don't happen overnight. That things take time to develop. Well, I have also heard that saying, "Shit happens." I wanted to play the blues, because I felt the blues. It was a way of starting over from the beginning. It was an opportunity to retrace my life—a chance to change my old patterns. So I joined a rock group again. I began to learn self-control and to look at music as fun again. Just like when I was a fan of rock groups like the Rolling Stones.

I had it rough in the Ramones, but that was all over now. At least it gave me a good background from which to judge my mistakes. I began to think that I could survive another round with rock'n'roll music. I knew it would take its toll. I was under no illusions. I didn't know if there was anyone in the music business who cared whether I ever played another note of rock'n'roll again.

One of the things I realized was that the whole competitive thing about being in a band was boring. I wish all of us in the

Surviving the Ramones

Ramones could have been cool, but we didn't know any better. We let the business push us around. It's a system that controls rebellion for profit, sort of like drug lords do. Originally, maybe it was different. Did Chuck Berry's "Roll Over Beethoven" stand for that?

It's hard getting a band started. I remember when I was in Gary Kurfirst's office discussing the musicians that might be available to start a band, he didn't have a good word to say about anyone. I don't want to mention any names, but he ran everyone down. Well, I could tell there was nothing happening. All he wanted was for me to write some Ramones songs for their next album.

Aggression is what drives a great rock'n'roll band. It can't be faked or it will be obvious crap. Upper-class people can't understand that. The capitalist system can't create rock'n'roll bands and expect everybody to accept that as rebellion. That won't work. A system that protects one side, while the rest of us do time, is going to make me mad. So don't expect me to cooperate.

I was never even aware that there was a class system in America, until I moved to Ann Arbor, Michigan. This town was populated—dominated might be a better description—by rich, spoiled college students. One of the things that had attracted me there was the myth that high energy rock'n'roll came from Ann Arbor. I can still see how Liverpool gave us the Beatles, but I'll never figure out how Ann Arbor gave us Iggy and the Stooges.

Going to Tower Records every day kept my spirits up, but there was pretty much nothing to do there. I guess that's why

LOBOTOMY

I started to play the guitar again. I started out like everyone else, by learning old blues numbers, I thought I was going to be the next Johnny Winter or something. But I am what I am. I still just shake and smack the guitar around up there like Johnny Ramone does. I don't bother to play it. I think I use it to yell at everybody.

Since there was a blues jam in Ann Arbor at the Blind Pig every Sunday, I went there to see what was happening. Soon I started going there faithfully and jamming with the locals. On one occasion, I was just trying to mind my own business, struggling to get through an old Muddy Waters tune I had learned from a blues cassette that I had stolen from a local Ann Arbor band's rehearsal room. When I ended the tune, Al Vicious, the bass player with the house band just stood there grinning, trying to be polite. The drummer and the harp player didn't know what to do, so I played it cool. I don't think anyone there thought that the blues should be played that dirty, but they were amazed and still wanted to see me do something.

Gary, who runs the jam at the Pig, came to my rescue. He strolled up to the bandstand, trying to make out like every-thing that was happening had actually been planned. He took the mike and announced that I would play "Wart Hog" for everyone. *What the fuck?* I thought to myself. I counted out "One, two, three, four," and we started cranking it out. Everybody went home happy.

Back in the early eighties, my counselor at Odyssey House, Harold Holloway, tried very hard to reach me, but

Surviving the Ramones

wasn't getting anywhere. Harold knew I was about at the end
of my line. A lot of other therapists would have given me up
as a lost cause, but he tried his best. Finally, he tried to get
me to write a love song to get me in touch with my feelings.
He kept after me until I panicked. Finally, I knew I had to
give him something.

You want a song. I'll give you a song, I thought to myself.

The next day I gave him the lyrics to "Wart Hog":

> *I take some dope I feel so sick*
> *It's a sick world, sick, sick, sick*
> *Doomsday visions of junkies and fags*
> *Artificial phonies, I hate it, hate it*
>
> *Death, death, death is the price I pay*
> *It's a sick world, what can I say*
> *No such thing as an even break*
> *It's stealing and cheating, take, take, take*
>
> *Wart, wart hog*
> *Wart, wart hog*
> *Wart, wart hog*
> *Wart, wart hog*
>
> *I wanna puke I can't sit still*
> *Just took some dope and I feel ill*
> *It's a sick world, sick, sick, sick*
> *It's a hopeless life, I hate it, hate it*

LOBOTOMY

"What the fuck is this?" Harold asked me, looking at the piece of paper I had just given him.

"I don't really know," I replied.

I could tell he was pissed off. On my way out, I think I heard him say to himself, "Why are they all such knuckle-heads?"

Well, anyway, on my way home that night at the blues jam, after I had just finished playing "Wart Hog," I felt myself getting the fever again. I could feel that old love of the spotlight stirring in me, so I started weighing the odds. If you do it, it hurts you. And if you don't do it, it hurts you. So there's not really a choice, I thought. Also, if I had a group, I'd have some people to hang out with again. I was lonely, bored, and needed something to do. Finally I decided to do it. *What the fuck*, I thought to myself. I knew I could depend on Tom Templin, a local bruiser, to keep the band in line. Tom was from Detroit, so I thought I'd look for my new band members there. It was scary, but I knew I was going to do it. There was no turning back unless I wanted to be all alone, I still have to run with my own kind, and that's why I started The Chinese Dragons, and wouldn't you know it, I ended up singing "Wart Hog" every night again! What a goof.

For good measure I decided upon a "fuck everybody" attitude, and after a while I thought I'd play some Ramones songs and fit some blues songs into my show. *Wow, this is great*, I thought. I was excited.

Before I went upstairs to my flat, I called an associate of mine at the Doug McAlpine agency from a pay phone near where I lived.

"Hi, Doug, it's Dee Dee. How ya' doing?"

"How are things?" Doug said.

"Oh, everything's ok. Well, listen to this. I'm going to start a rock'n'roll band again and it's going to be from Detroit, like Iggy and the Stooges and the MC5."

"Wow," Doug said, "that's really something."

"Yeah, I know, it's going to be great."

Doug was an expert at blues and stuff like that. I met him at Solley's, a cocktail lounge in Dearborn, Michigan, where the blues bands play. He always tried to be polite, as he was trying to be now, but I could tell that was as far as I was going to get with him, even though he did get the Chinese Dragons their first gig at Solley's. I thought it was really cool for us to play a real blues club.

How it all happened though, was through Jeff Grant, a local guitar legend from Detroit. I met Jeff at a Jim McCarty

LOBOTOMY

and the Detroit Blues Band concert at the Paycheck Lounge in Hamtramck. Jeff took a liking to me, and started showing me around Ferndale, and I got to know the area around the Pay-Less drugstore, the Loving Touch Massage Parlor, and the Coney Island place, where the Chinese Dragons and I would later go every night for dinner.

Jeff Grant had a little rehearsal room in Ferndale, not far from Gordy's Guitar Shop. He brought me up there one night after we had been painting the town red. We had just come from Centerfold's, a local go-go bar, and we were both tipsy and feeling good. When we got upstairs, Richie, Allen, and Scott were up there. Allen was as drunk as a skunk, and Richie and Scott seemed to be on another planet. This is great, I thought.

"You guys wanna play?"

"What do you wanna do?" they asked.

"Oh, I don't know."

And that's how the Chinese Dragons started. It was about time Detroit stuck another rowdy rock'n'roll band in the universe, and I was glad to be on board.

So I got another chance to do what I've always done. I guess "Wart Hog" is my way of yelling at everyone who comes to my shows. People look at me with glee, but also like I am crazy, when I sing that song.

Buenos Aires

When I went to South America the last time around

with my new band, I had a bunch of little creatures with

Ramones T-shirts on, following me everywhere I went. As

soon as I stepped out of the elevator and into the lobby of the

fancy hotel I was staying at in downtown Buenos Aires, they

were shouting questions at me, demanding autographs, and

LOBOTOMY

asking me to pose for photos. I would feel myself start to flip, but I didn't lose it, and I didn't do any yelling, even at reception, or at the sneaky security guards patrolling the halls. I was imprisoned in the hotel room again, but this time I wasn't chained down by a cocaine hangover. I'd come a long way. I even went down to the pool and sat there under one of those umbrellas in the sun, and tried to relax.

I could have had all the cocaine I wanted, but I turned it down. I am just happy I don't have to suffer like that any more. Then I started to feel very gleeful that my idea of a party is a little more jaded than when I first came to South America. Actually, the thought that I was going to make some money for a change was a big kick to me. I had a laugh. *Boy, am I nuts*, I thought to myself. Well, I guess that's what makes me so lovable.

Going back to Buenos Aires with my new band, I couldn't believe how loved the Ramones were. Their music is a very intense influence on the kids down there. I guess because the Ramones and their fans come from the same sort of situations. Certainly not the same situation some spoiled student is coming from in Ann Arbor. Then I could tell that if the Ramones were put into the position of representing something of learning value, it is that there is hope and that it is possible to rise above oppression. That kind of stuff really makes me know that it's worth it to keep playing in a band.

In Argentina, I sneaked out of the hotel and got caught by a load of kids who surrounded me and started asking me questions. We sat down on the stoop, just like I used to with my "brudders" in Forest Hills a long time ago. We got talking

Surviving the Ramones

about the Ramones and stuff, and then the conversation turned to guitars.

"Dee Dee," one of them said. "You play guitar in the old style."

Then one of them asked me what it was like when I first started playing.

"Well, you know, we used to get one of those old guitars and clamp a pick-up on it, then plug it in our mom's stereo when no one was home."

They couldn't believe it.

"That's what we do too, Dee Dee."

Christ, is this 1964 or 1992? I thought.

We went to the theater to do a show for TV. It was a riot. During a break in taping, I wandered off to the side of the stage and hid behind the curtain and spied on the other band that was on the bill. From what I could tell, they seemed very New York–influenced. They had a Johnny Thunders–type on guitar; counted "one, two, three, four," like the Ramones; and sounded like the Pistols. When I saw the singer's broken teeth, I knew where they were coming from.

Dee Dee with Kessie in
Germany, 1995
Barbara Zampini

Dee Dee with Kessie,
Amsterdam, 1995
Barbara Zampini

Somehow, the last thing I needed was to get

involved with any more insensitive music business types,

like the promoter based in Nihagen, who first invited me to

the Netherlands where I formed a somewhat messy musi-

cal project called ICLC. I was on my own, and for nine

months I lived in a cheap hotel room in the Rembrandt, next

LOBOTOMY

to the train station in Venlo, a small border town in Holland. I liked Venlo, but I could tell it didn't like me. It was made very obvious to me. So, I moved again, this time to Amsterdam.

My first apartment in Amsterdam was on Rosen Straat. Amsterdam is a beautiful, tree-lined village-like city. It has a very free spirit, and it's not a place to go and try to get serious. But that's what I did, and it didn't work. The apartment on Rosen Straat had a machine shop underneath it. The drilling was driving me mad. I piled carpet after carpet on the floor to try to deaden the noise. I found used carpets in the garbage that dogs had shit on too many times, and took them to the dry cleaner. After a good washing, they were completely reusable. The noise from the street, as well as the sound of yelling children from the playground downstairs filled my apartment all day long and steadily shattered my nerves. Finally, in an all-out effort to block out the noise I went to the Block Hamm department store in the Haag, and bought some rolls of transparent blue-plastic tape, with which I wrapped up the whole inside of the apartment.

The tension got to be too much for me, and I had to move again. I got a new apartment on Harten Straat. That didn't turn out to be much better. It wasn't exactly the street where I was living that was bad. It was the whole city. I realized then that maybe the whole European attitude toward Americans is pretty bad.

After two years in Holland, I didn't make one single friend. It got so bad in Amsterdam that in the summer, if I wanted to get out of the apartment for a while for some air, the best place to go was to sit on the edge of the sidewalk next to the canal and try to hide myself from the passing American-hating citizens of Amsterdam.

To make things worse, the Ramones were still together. They even did a live show on MTV while I was living in Amsterdam. It seemed like any little thing they did ended up causing me grief. They looked horrible on MTV—so old, tired, and angry. Even though, I hadn't had anything to do with them, it was hard to get that Ramones stamp off your head, for some reason. I guess it's the curse of fame. After the show on MTV people started making smart-aleck remarks to me around town. Why does Joey seem so fucked up? What is he on? Why didn't he sing? Why did CJ sing? and so on. The general opinion in Amsterdam was, "Why do they bother any more?"

Then they went and booked a date in Rotterdam and everybody was asking me if I could put them on the guest list. Can you imagine that? Two beautiful Dutch girls even tried to pick me up and trick me into having sex with them. I couldn't believe it. They wanted to be with me so they could get to meet Joey Ramone! I was getting sick of so many girls doing that to me. Even my new girlfriend, Barbara, was a big Ramones fan. She even named all her toy dolls and animals Dee Dee when she was in Buenos Aires. She really wanted to go to Rotterdam to see them play.

I had met Barbara on my previous tour of Argentina—she was from Buenos Aires. Eventually she flew out to Holland and joined me in Amsterdam, after much wrangling with her parents, and with the authorities about residence permits. After all, she was very young. In the end she had just about persuaded me to go to the show in Rotterdam, when we

LOBOTOMY

Dee Dee and Barbara
the year they met, 1994

received a Ramones fanzine in the mail. In it was an interview with Johnny Ramone and they asked him if the
Ramones ever did a last show together, would they have me
come up on stage and play with them.

"No," he replied, "CJ is our bass player now."

Well that was true and I wasn't instigating anything about
playing a last show with the Ramones, but the show in
Rotterdam was rumored to be their last. So, everybody in town
started hassling me to go play with them. It was insane. In the
end I let it be known that I would be in New York the day they
were playing in Rotterdam. I also told them that I would, however, be in Rotterdam to hang out afterwards. It was all very
touchy because they wanted more songs from me again.

Instead I took Barbara to the Milky Way, the Milkweg, a club
I had played with the Ramones on a number of occasions. By
now I was getting used to the dirty looks and strange treatment

that I received when I went out. I guess it didn't help having a beautiful young girlfriend when you're forty-three years old, but that's my style. What can you do, right? Amsterdam felt like my last stand. I had been on the run for five years since I quit the Ramones, and I was tired of running.

As soon as Barbara and I got comfortable by the bar, a horrible, creepy young little girl slithered up to me and said:

"Are you like Bill Wyman, the loser of the Rolling Stones?"

"I really don't throw sweets to babies," I replied. I was really just trying to get away from her, but she was clever. She was right in my face, trying to stare me down, waiting for my reaction so she could get a good giggle from it all.

Well, I looked at her hardened, mean, little-girl face, and I attacked. I got in the first giggle, with a finely executed, bittersweet smirk that I have often practiced. Then I brought my hand up to my mouth, cupped it, and let go with a cough into her face, and then added, "You must be the loser of the Milkweg."

Then I spun around on my heels and smart-marched Barbara in the opposite direction, so as to regain my composure.

"I've had enough. Come on, baby. Let's go home," I said.

I promised I would take her to see the Ramones at CBGB's in New York. I happened to know they were playing there again to make some money to pay Marc and CJ and the road crew, and a few other band bills.

On the way out of the Milkweg, I heard an angry voice curse me in Dutch. As I turned around I saw it was that same creepy bitch who had just ranked on me about Bill Wyman. Well, if they can't be nice, then why should I be? That's the way it goes. Did they expect to push me around and that I was going to end up all friendly? No way. Maybe Bob Hope would, but not Dee Dee Ramone. No way! I can't wish anyone luck if they can't wish me any.

"The next time the Ramones play Rotterdam, I'll put you on the train and send you backstage to meet Joey Ramone, ok?" I told the little creep as we exited the premises. Of course, I wasn't telling the truth, but this was getting to be a goof for me.

I told her that the pinhead who brings out the Gabba Gabba Hey sign is still worth seeing! That pinhead will never leave them! He's got the John Merrick lifestyle—fame and pinhead bitches to boot.

Finally I said, "You know what though, you creep? You would be blessed if you could get up close and kiss his pointy head! Now get lost!"

Barbara and I walked along the Keizersgraft (graft means *canal* in Dutch) to our little apartment on Hartenstrat, the stars were all out, and the sky was beautiful. I felt ok. "What a *lovely* evening," I said.

Barbara asked me, "What did you do after you played your last show with the Ramones?"

"Well," I said to her in an almost fatherly way, "you know what I did? After I put my bass down for the last time, I walked over to the pinhead and rubbed its head for good luck. And that was it. I hope my dear brothers do the same thing. They're going to be needing all the luck they can get."

As I walked the rest of the way home I suddenly said, "You know what? I do feel lucky. How could everything turn out so well for someone like me? It's amazing!"

Mechelen

A year had gone by since that walk back from the Milky

Way. Finally, I had to get me and Barbara out of

Amsterdam. Another American couple we met told us that

the only way they could survive living there was to try and

stay invisible. I could relate to that. I wasn't happy about it.

I felt like I'd been tarred and feathered and run out of town.

LOBOTOMY

As a result I moved to Mechelen near Antwerp in Belgium with Barbara and two dogs we had acquired along the way, Kessie and Babita. Kessie was a mean street dog and very grouchy. Kessie also hated Amsterdam, and was always acting up on the street. Back in Argentina Barbara had a pit bull named Doogie, so after a while, I decided that I'd better get another dog. We got Babita, who was some kind of small Doberman and Rotweiler mixture.

I could have been very happy in Mechelen. True, it was boring, but we had a nice place to live and it was quiet. It's sort of like the Ann Arbor/Detroit, area of the US. It's very strange being a New Yorker in Mechelen. It's sort of medieval

Dee Dee with Babita,
Amsterdam, 1995
Barbara Zampini

there. Cathedrals, cobblestone streets, hand-painted signs, coats of arms, and on Sundays there's absolutely no signs of life.

Also, the Belgian people are a lot friendlier than the Dutch. However, the Belgian police are a bunch of sick bastards—they were on my case almost as soon as I got there. They acted a bit like how I always imagined the really roughnecked southern state troopers were like in Alabama during the height of racial tensions in the deep south during the '60s.

As soon as I moved to Mechelen, I got a lawyer in Antwerp to get me a residence permit. He suggested that for $10,000, I could start a publishing company that would qualify me for a permit in Belgium. It sounded good to me. I was happy, and said, "Ok, let's do it." Michael from Herzog and Strauss immediately sent my lawyer all the papers, but he presumably never got started on my case. His grouchy assistant told me that she had filed Barbara and me on a police report, and that we would be ok until the papers came in. I asked her if we should leave Belgium first, to make things legal. "No," she snobbishly replied. "Stay here in Belgium where you are safe."

Safe, my ass, as I later found out. The only people who really ever seem to know the law are the police.

I had that worried feeling. I could sense trouble was coming my way, and as usual, I was right. Barbara and I were almost deported from Belgium. One morning the cops picked us up in Mechelen when we were coming out of the newsagent with the morning papers. For no reason at all,

LOBOTOMY

they just forced us into their patrol car and took us to the station. They would not let me call a lawyer. They seemed so full of unnecessary hatred toward me and Barbara. They threatened us. They gave us an alternative—you can go to the USSR or Czechoslovakia, but you are on the computer with a violation of the laws of the European Community. We had to go. We lost everything we owned. I did not have any drugs on me—I didn't do them at all any more. I didn't have a weapon on me. I hadn't even committed a traffic offense.

My lawyer in Amsterdam told me that I was picked up for nothing, that the cops in Mechelen are like that. He told me that no American would be safe living there. I quite agree with him now. I have also learned my lesson and will never repeat that same mistake again. I will never go back to Belgium.

THEN, ONE day my mother called. It was weird. I hadn't spoken to her in at least four years. My ex-management in New York gave her my number.

She sounded all right, and I was glad she called. I told her that I wished that I could go back to Germany to live, but it was hard because I needed a residence permit and couldn't get one. She couldn't help. She lost her German citizenship and couldn't live there for more than six months a year any more. She gave me my grandmother's number in Berlin, and I called her. She really sounded off the wall.

I could really see now why my mother was like she was when I was younger. Going through World War II, the bomb raids, the Russian invasion, her family, my father for a husband, it couldn't have been easy for her. Oh, and I hate to admit it—for her to have *me* for a son. But whatever sympathies I have for her, the wall around my emotions will always be there. I ended up telling her that my family is the Ramones. That I am Dee Dee Ramone, not Douglas Colvin. I never was much of a family man. Still, I felt all right about talking to her and after we hung up I bet we both felt the same way. All she or I can depend on is ourselves.

Barbara and Dee Dee's mother, Miami
Dee Dee Ramone

Epilogue

I am sitting in a room now. It isn't mine. I am in Argentina again. A sleepy neighborhood in Buenos Aires called Banfield, at my girlfriend's grandmother's house. I am hiding again because I am feeling miserable and I know I will only make anyone else miserable who sees me, so I am giving all concerned a break. I do something stupid and let a dog wander in here, thinking he might cheer me up. I met him outside by the gate, and I have already given him the name Ramone. He's a fat old street dog that has obviously been in a fight with another dog and has a slightly wounded leg. I have a slightly wounded head. I have had a fight with a Ramones' fan.

Barbara's grandmother and her two sisters met us at the airport. They put us up in Barbara's sister's room—she ended up sleeping in the living room. It got a bit edgy right away. I think I might even have driven everybody out of their minds, so here I am, sitting alone again, in a room, writing. When I try to walk into the outside, the world gets too intense for me. It makes me cringe. I feel vulnerable, out of place, and unwelcome everywhere I go. I feel shitty, like a criminal would feel, except I am not a criminal.

At this point, Ramone, the dog that I let in here, gets up and exits the room. He maneuvered his way in here. Ramone had to get his way. So I let him in. I wish he would appreciate it. Instead, I got caught up in the inside, thinking about outside. I know Ramone is just an old abused dog, and how would he know what's happening, but it still bothers me. You fat bastard, I mutter under my breath as he duckwalks out the door.

What I needed most now was a visa for Barbara, so we could go to America, where I felt that we would both be better off. But that would take another year of trying over and over. It was difficult. She was underaged and had an Argentinian passport, and her parents wouldn't help us without major struggles. The red tape you go through in Argentina is rough.

Surviving the Ramones

In Argentina, it's like a time warp. It reminds me of when America was a nice country to live in. Even though everything is harder in Argentina, the people are nicer there than in most places. The air is so smoggy that it cuts up your lungs. Bus drivers there are out to kill. They purposefully try to push people on mopeds off the highway with their big smelly buses. It's a madhouse. Everybody is blowing clouds of black smoke out of their exhaust pipes into each other's open car windows. Everybody's car window is open because no one has air-conditioning. The cars there are all old and fucked up, but have a lot of soul. It's very funky.

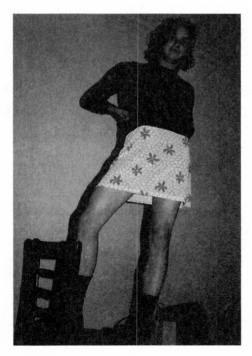

Barbara at the
Chelsea Hotel, 1996
Dee Dee Ramone

LOBOTOMY

The hassles become mucho to get money to live on in Argentina. My accountant, Ira, used to send me money via the Western Union on Cordoba and Suipacha. The cab ride to get there was always a nightmare. First of all, it was hot. Very, very hot. Then, the cab driver would start chattering in Spanish nonstop about the Ramones. I can't understand a word. I mutter "sí," to him once in a while. I am trying to keep my head, but since my driver's head is always turning around to talk to me and his eyes are never on the road ahead, I keep a fixed glare out the front windshield, sort of trying to will the taxi through the maze of traffic, determined that we won't fuck up and have an accident, because I have to get the money. The traffic is bumper to bumper. Stop and go. Nut-job angry Latin drivers. It's like in a movie.

There are also police roadblocks along the highway. When I get to Western Union, I run in and come right out with six 100-peso notes. I jump back in the cab and head back to Banfield on the outskirts of Buenos Aires, my current address. I should be happy, but I never get any peace.

AS WE'RE driving along, the news came on the radio that the Ramones are due to play their last show in Buenos Aires on March 16. Iggy is also on the bill. Something always ruins everything. Right now it's the rock and pop station. They are advertising the Iggy and the Ramones show nonstop.

Then there's an announcement that Attack 77 have been added to the show. This really sucks. I'm not in the mood to see Attack 77 or Iggy's stupid face, or John, Joey, and Marky's stupid faces either. And, as soon as I am out of the taxi, I storm back inside my place and turn off rock and pop, which Barbara has on full blast on a Panasonic boombox. What a shitty day. It's also a blow that the Ramones might be sticking around for a rematch. What a drag it all was.

It was becoming obvious that I was under some obligation to everyone to try to play at the final show with the Ramones. Everybody in the neighborhood started pestering me for tickets. I had to take out my guitar and play a few Ramones songs for everybody on the sidewalk in front of my home to keep the peace. It was horrible for me. I was really becoming demoralized. By the time the Ramones landed at Buenos Aires International for their last-ever show, I was wishing I was dead. I ended up promising to try and get people free Ramones tickets. I called Rock and Pop, the Ramones' promoter in Buenos Aires, nine times. I spoke with a few different people there. They couldn't promise me anything, except that they would call me back. They never did, so I guessed I wasn't going to go to the concert. That I had called Rock and Pop nine times and they were so rude made me feel like the whole world was against me. What else could I think?

There was a lot of anger surrounding the show before it even happened. There was a riot in downtown Buenos Aires, when a ticket giveaway was inexplicably ignored by the promoter of the concert. None of the winners got their free tickets, after they had been standing in line all night to wait for them, so they got angry. It really made me not want to go after that.

I saw the whole thing. I had just been to Western Union to get some money and was on my way to the Dunkin Donuts store to buy six tickets for Barbara's sisters Sofia and Rocio and their friends. The fact of having to buy the six Ramones tickets made me feel funny—I didn't know that they would be giving tickets away next door at the Coca-Cola building. By the time the police arrived to clear everybody out, every store window was broken. Later on, the riot was reported on MTV.

Then Monte finally called me. After that I got to speak on the phone with Johnny Ramone.

"I don't know how we got stuck doing the Metallica tour, Dee Dee," he was going. "I am half crazy. Everybody's blown out. Arturo got busted for something right before we left for Brazil. It's been a nightmare. I wish you would come to the show. We'd like to see you."

"Ok," I said. I felt terrible after I got off the phone with him. Despite all my troubles, I felt sorry for John and the rest of the Ramones.

I arrived at their hotel at five o'clock, the time that Monte had arranged to meet me. The band and I were going to do "53rd & 3rd" together at the concert. We were going to go over the song at soundcheck and then go for dinner and hang out.

This all sounded fine. What they didn't know is that for the last couple of days I had been trying to get inside the American Embassy to get a visa for Barbara, so I could take her to New York. I started my day at five in the morning, as I had to be waiting in line outside the Embassy by six. I might be crazy, I don't know. Whatever I am, I am not a good loser. I will fight and fight for what I want. People always say about me "Oh, Dee Dee, he always gets his way."

Surviving the Ramones

My mother and I have some kind of evil German clandestine arrangement—believe me, it wasn't my father who taught me how to fight. Finally, I was at such a loss that I called her up and said, "Mom, what should I do?"

"Go in there and fight and yell, that's what I did at the Embassy in Florida, Dee Dee. Then they paid attention to me, and I got my way."

THAT'S WHAT I did. The day of the Ramones show, I went to the Embassy first thing in the morning. It was already crowded. I walked up and down the sidewalk casing the line a few times, but my nerve was up. I marched myself right up to the cop guarding some sort of mysterious bunkerlike entrance through the gate.

"I want to go in there and get a visa," I demanded.

When I was at the second electronic search gate, I tried to slip them 300 pesos, but they wouldn't accept.

"We don't do that any more, señor," they said.

What got me the visa eventually was yelling just like my mother had told me to do. I should have had a party to celebrate, but I had the taxi let me off in front of the Hyatt Hotel to meet the Ramones. Because of the crowds, the driver would not stop. I had to open the door and jump out. I paid him later when I got back to Banfield. Barbara, who was not supposed to come, was right behind me. It was too much.

The hotel was fenced off by a security gate. There were police everywhere. Fans all over the place. The promoters were outside the hotel. They saw me and gave me a dirty look. Still, I tried to attract their attention.

LOBOTOMY

"It's Dee Dee," I shouted. "It's me."

All the Ramones fans started agreeing, and shouting "It's Dee Dee. It's Dee Dee. Let him in." But they were pulling me back away from the gate and demanding autographs and photos.

The police were glaring at me with pure hatred. Everybody started to bum's rush me. It was like a tidal wave coming at me. By chance, I spotted Marky. I tried to get his attention. "Marky, help me!" I shouted.

He pretended not to see me. He was hiding behind the dark Elvis-type sunglasses he was wearing. He had spun a web of hate around himself. With his black wig, black motorcycle jacket on, and his pale white skin, he looked so much like the original Marky Ramone that it was unreal.

He was standing outside the hotel, protected from the fans by the security gate. When the Ramones fans saw him, they flipped. I was out there alone. It was obvious that Monte had arranged for them to sign autographs at the same time as he had told me to be at the hotel. I had to fight for my life. It was horrible. Somehow I squashed Barbara and myself between the security guards, the police, and the fans. I was dodging sharp pencils and pens being thrust toward my eyes by autograph seekers, and then someone kicked me in the shins. When I finally made it into the hotel lobby, I was pissed off.

Marky was the first person I saw.

"I hate you," I shouted. "You saw me, and didn't let me in."

"It's not true. I didn't see you, Dee Dee, bunny chicken. Kiss me. We love you."

Surviving the Ramones

This sucks, I thought to myself.

Monte was there. He looked real blown out. It was sad to see him like that. Marc was trying to smile. It was that Hollywood showbiz practiced look-of-concern smile that makes me feel even crazier when I look at Marc's crazy face. I was losing my grip. He's as insane as Monte, I thought to myself.

I saw Johnny Ramone and I was quite taken aback. This is serious, I thought. He looked very, very bad. Really terrible. Very blown out. I felt horrible about what I was seeing. This is not right. I was concerned about Johnny Ramone in the same way I was about Brian James a few years ago when he did the final tour with the Damned. Soon I pulled myself together, and started to feel more cheerful. This is great, I thought. Barbara and I ended up having dinner with them in the lounge area of the hotel. A few privileged Ramones fans got to pester me while I tried to eat and talk to a worn-out Joey.

"Dee Dee," Marc asked me, "what did you order?"

"Oh, you know, Marc," I replied, "a steak sandwich and French onion soup. The most expensive things on the menu. You know, Marc, trying to get the most out of it as I can."

"I know what you mean, bro," he lovingly confided to me. I could tell that under his calm demeanor, Marc was secretly planning a comeback some day.

It made me feel good. How could I dislike this guy, I thought. After dinner, I went to the soundcheck in the van with the promoter and the rest of the band, except for Johnny Ramone, who was too miserable to be with Joey and

LOBOTOMY

Marc, so he went alone in a car with Eddie Vedder and his friends.

When they got to the stadium where they would be playing for 90,000 people, everything was ready for them. They took their positions and started checking. The group might have seemed impressive to other people, but not to me. They were good, but they had lost their cool. Johnny Ramone seemed more like a tennis player than a guitar player.

In the end, I didn't stay for the show. I hadn't exactly received the royal treatment from the Ramones, their fans, or Rock and Pop. I tried to be good about a real bad situation— to remain loyal after all the aggravation I had been through. But it didn't work. Fuck them, I thought to myself. On the way back to the hotel, I opened the door of the van and as soon as we stopped for a red light, I jumped out. I hailed a cab and before anyone knew what had happened, I was on my way back to Banfield, to Barbara's grandmother's house. Her sisters, Sofia and Rocio, were fighting so bitterly over the four tickets that I had given them and who would go with who, that I gave the other two tickets that Rock and Pop had given me to them to keep the peace. So I didn't go to the show. Instead I listened to it in my kitchen on the radio, tapping nervously with my nails on a red linoleum-topped table.

I felt there was no excuse for the way I had been treated. It was pretty inconsiderate to ask me to go to the show to play a song with them, set a time to meet me, and then take no responsibility for what happened outside the hotel when I went to meet them.

Surviving the Ramones

So many of these weak-handshake type of incidents had left me very bitter towards the fans and the Ramones. There was so much harassment in the band about a possible Ramones documentary that was supposed to be filmed around their last performance, that I left them to it—left them my phone number and said I would make myself available. Somehow I knew it would never happen.

ONE OF the last times I saw Johnny, I met him at a coffee shop on 24th Street. And I knew how it would be. He tries to take over your life, tell you what to believe, what to do. He barely spoke with me, and when I got up to leave he said, "Dee Dee, where are you going?"

And I said, "Listen, I'm going."

MY FATHER died a few years ago. He had moved back to the States and had gotten into a very bad accident which left him on a life-support system. I had made my mind that I couldn't get back at the guy, but I didn't feel like I was his son.

I had all these fantasies about making the family good, bringing my mother and my sister together with my wife Barbara. I desperately wanted to make something more for Barbara; she was young and I hoped my mother would like her. It wasn't a good idea. My mother was plain crazy.

A RAMONES story can't really have a happy ending. I'm just glad it's over with, though some of it was fun. I really don't think the Ramones should play together again. I say that not

LOBOTOMY

out of meanness; it's actually out of concern for them, and myself. I wish everyone in the band good luck. Because of our relationships with each other, we're all damaged. We hurt each other. My book tells the story—it's some story and I'm glad I told it.

I have my memories, though. Like the time we played that New Year's Eve show, with the Heartbreakers. Wayne County was the DJ, and I used to really like Wayne. I went up there into the DJ booth with him and we started snooping around, and we found a pistol. I stood there holding the pistol, talking about the Searchers. I thought, *This is so crazy.*

Then I walked home, from 29th Street to 2nd Avenue. It must have been 5:30 in the morning. I snuck away so that I didn't have to carry the amps! I could've gotten a ride with everybody in the van, but I just left by myself.

New Year's Eve and there I am, walking alone in the freezing cold. And I was happy. I thought, Boy, man, we got to play with a big group, the Heartbreakers.

That was probably the ending of that glitter scene, the New York rock scene. The scene that had that look. The breaking of rock'n'roll traditions. And not thinking that you had to *be* it or *work* for it. You just had to *shout* and *demand* it.

And it was great. Because it gave everybody a chance to say something. That's revolution.

On Sire Records:

Ramones (1976)

Ramones Leave Home (1977)

Rocket to Russia (1977)

Road to Ruin (1978)

Rock'n'Roll High School (1979)

End of the Century (1980)

Pleasant Dreams (1981)

Subterranean Jungle (1983)

Too Tough to Die (1984)

Animal Boy (1986)

Halfway to Sanity (1987)

RamonesMania (1988)

Brain Drain (1989)

All the Stuff and More Volume 1 (1990)

All the Stuff and More Volume 2 (1991)

On Warner Brothers Records

It's Alive (1979)

On Chrysalis Records

Loco Live (1991)

On Radioactive Records

Mondo Bizarro (1992)

On Rhino Records

Hey! Ho! Let's Go! The Anthology: Box Set (1999)